# Patrick H. McNamara

# More Than Money

## Portraits of Transformative Stewardship

Foreword by M. Douglas Meeks

An Alban Institute Publication

Library of Congress Card Number 99-73547
ISBN 1-56699-215-X

*To*

*My Mother*

*Agnes Hayes McNamara*

*with love*

# CONTENTS

Patrick McNamara is a seasoned sociologist with a conviction held in an unusually and refreshingly strong way: He believes Christian stewardship can be rehabilitated. He fully realizes how troubled stewardship is in the ailing mainline denominations, but he refuses cynicism from whatever quarter or for whatever reason. He even chides theological approaches that give up on the language of stewardship. Whence this hopefulness about stewardship?

McNamara does not engage in biblical and theological arguments but is rather a close observer of eleven congregations that had been identified to him broadly as "stewardship churches." He set out to discover why these churches deserved that billing. In other words, he looked at the actual practices of congregations who are hopeful about stewardship. This book is an exciting narrative about what is actually happening in these churches. The reader will find here not a flat functional report that skims the surface but rather an engaged discernment of the theological, spiritual, pastoral, liturgical, and diaconal reality that undergirds the stewardship of these congregations. And thus we end up with a serious theological claim lived out: The hope for stewardship stems from the presence of the giving God who makes possible the giving of God's people.

The reader should not expect here an easy, five-step stewardship program. Each of the eleven congregations studied is unique. The author artfully catches the distinctive character, setting, and challenges of each congregation. Moreover, he constantly makes clear that the "stewardship approach" must be contextualized in the differences and particularities of each congregation. Nevertheless, he does think that some traits common to a stewardship approach do emerge, even if he refuses to propound easy criteria for "success" on the basis of them. In fact, the point of a stewardship approach is not success in numbers but a process, a way of congregational living, that changes people and their life relationships. It is infinitely more important to assist the Holy Spirit in creating stewards than simply to concoct annual stewardship "drives." An approach that is truly transformative of people and communities rests in the Spirit's vivification of the congregation. And so McNamara gives us narratives of struggle, hopefulness, and at times, wonderful faithfulness.

At least five common characteristics (though contextualized differently in each setting) emerge from the narratives. First, all the congregations work at a *theology of stewardship* and resist defining it in terms of secularized benevolence and philanthropy. Stewardship is not a euphemism for fund-raising. Nor is it grounded in a "pay-back" theology defined by society's notions of exchange. The theology of stewardship in these congregations is not mere motivational rhetoric in support of fundraising but an overall inspirational paradigm guiding pastor and congregation. Common to these congregations is the awareness that the gospel is a countercultural and deeply troubling message in which "the very meaning of money, wealth, one's time priorities, all of which we come to regard in our culture as a highly personal possession, is profoundly challenged." It is a narrative that goes against the grain of consumer culture governed by the logic of commodity exchange. God's sovereignty is over all gifts that we have received, not just money and possessions. The key is the coequal importance of giving time, talents, and money—which means, simply put, the return of our lives to God. The outcome is a freedom arising from returning generously the excessive generosity of God in the gift of Jesus Christ.

Second, all the congregations reveal the *importance of pastoral leadership* fore genuine stewardship. But the author notes that the stewardship approach runs counter to conventional notions and rhetoric about pastoral responsibility. The approach is a dialogical model of partnership rather than a parenting model that leads to dependency. The congregations expect their pastors to be attuned to the needs of congregations for meaning, healing, and a sense of the sacred. But they look for pastoral leadership that inspires and offers resources for lay leaders, and empowers church members to forsake dependency and become intentional about the allocation of time and money in their own ministry.

A third common characteristic is that these congregations emphasize the actual *experience of God's grace*. They do not expect people to express gratitude unless they have received grace. They do not construe grace as merely an intellectual or volitional reality. Therefore, these congregations know there will not be any real stewardship except it arise out of the means of grace: lively worship, encounter of God's word in Bible study, the experience of forgiveness. Only the passion of the gospel creates passion for self-giving. Everything depends on the unmistakable articulation of the gospel but in the idiom of the people. Music and liturgy also have to attend to the daily impressions and expressions of the people. These congregations do not look for one-time contributions of money but rather for the habits, dispositions, and virtues that express generous discipleship. Stewardship is the shape of discipleship that forms the household of Jesus Christ, a home for the homeless and a home for the generation of the generations.

Fourth, these congregations understand stewardship to be part and parcel of *commitment to service.* They encourage all members to be engaged in hands-on ministries of compassion and justice in the congregation and in the community. Christians who express their discipleship to Christ in the ministries and mission of the congregation become stewards who support their own ministry.

Finally, the members of these stewardship congregations are *bold in calling each other to give.* The call to give is not routinized but belongs to what people in the congregation owe each other: watching over each other in love. They ask each other to make a return by generous giving of oneself, one's resources, one's talents to extend the kingdom proclaimed by Christ. No one is without gifts from God to be given. The good steward finds the deepest joy in life in giving back what God has freely given.

The stories of these congregations will surely hearten all those who would hope for a faithful stewardship in our days.

*M. Douglas Meeks*
*Cal Turner Chancellor Professor of Theology and Wesleyan Studies*
*The Divinity School, Vanderbilt University*
*Nashville, Tennessee*

# ACKNOWLEDGMENTS

I am most grateful to those who initially supported my proposal that resulted in this book. Fred L. Hofheinz, program director for the Religion Division of the Lilly Endowment, was encouraging at every stage, from proposal through research and writing. Phil Williams, director of the Ecumenical Stewardship Center in Indianapolis, suggested the contacts at national offices of mainline denominations that yielded the names of the churches I studied. Editorial assistance came from my wife Joan (writing teacher supreme), and from Patricia Woods, professional editor and friendly critic. Special thanks go to the pastors of these fine churches whose warm welcomes and generous granting of interview time made my visits memorable and profitable. To their associate pastors, staffs, and committees as well, I acknowledge my indebtedness. I am especially grateful to Pam and Don Rondorf of Faith Lutheran Church in Seward, Nebraska; Marilyn Miller of First Presbyterian Church, Fort Worth, Texas; and Brian Hayes of All Saints Church (Episcopal), Pasadena, California. Finally, my heartfelt thanks to the superb editorial staff of the Alban Institute. Acquisitions editor Beth Ann Gaede proved a wise and encouraging guide throughout; Deborah Schnabel and David Lott provided helpful suggestions; Jean Caffey Lyles performed meticulous copyediting for which I am profoundly grateful.

# INTRODUCTION

If ever a word could make churchgoers' eyes glaze over, it's probably "stewardship." *Uh-oh. It's October. Here come the stewardship sermons.* Eyebrows go up as the pastor introduces the topic: "I dunno—sounds like another way of asking us for money." These reactions, of course, reflect the all-too-frequent identification of stewardship with fund-raising: the good steward is a church member conscientious about "supporting the church generously." Missing altogether are (1) awareness of stewardship as involving the giving of one's time and talent and (2) more basic by far, stewardship's essential spiritual ideals of receiving God's gifts and responding to those gifts by returning one's "time, talent, and treasure" to the service of God in this congregation. Inject these two themes, and stewardship embraces an inspiring theological vision. How could it be questioned?

Fact is, the vessel of stewardship rides on troubled waters today. When the most respected U.S. historian of stewardship, Robert Wood Lynn, turns skeptical after describing "the reasons for the meteoric rise of the stewardship movement"[1] and its heyday from the early 1900s through 1920, heads are bound to turn:

> "Stewardship," which once seemed to be a promising theological ideal upon which to base our giving, now means many different things to mainstream churchgoers. [If this is so], . . . does it mean anything in particular? Can it carry any authority? Perhaps it is time to question whether or not "stewardship" can work as today's dominant metaphor justifying and legitimating financial contributions to churches and other religious organizations.[2]

Lynn is joined by popular church consultant and author Loren Mead, who takes dead aim "at a most sacred cow." Churchgoers perceive stewardship "to be a euphemism for fundraising. This kind of double talk is genuinely confusing to many laypeople." The theology itself is suspect. Stewardship is "'pay-back' theology," urging church members to make a return to God, considering all the gifts he has given us. Stewardship has rarely been criticized so forcefully. Mead's broadside is pointed and personal:

> I yearn for a more complex and straight-talk theology of giving and of money that takes seriously the ambiguous character of my life, of my use of everything I have, and the straight-out sick way that I often relate to money and possessions as well as my whole life. Stewardship leaves out my sinfulness, my need for repentance, and the reality of the grace of God. I don't mind it as a simplistic theology, I just wish we had a theology of money and giving that had more substance.[3]

The word has been betrayed by church leaders trying to assure congregations that stewardship is really not about giving money to the church. Instead, they say, "it is about a relationship with God. [But] the charade has not worked."[4] When churchgoers hear stewardship, they think, "Give money."

Not far behind is historian and theologian John Mulder. Often, a theology of stewardship is based on the Christian doctrine of creation, a basis Mulder finds inadequate:

> God created the world; we are God's stewards; therefore, we give back to God what has been entrusted to us. Notably missing from the expressed motivations of most people who give to churches is one rooted in Christology: because of God's salvation in Jesus Christ, I respond in gratitude and give my money to God and the church.[5]

If, as church-giving research points out, most laypeople cannot remember hearing stewardship sermons, then stewardship theology fails to play much of a role in motivating people to give. Mulder thinks another approach (similar to Mead's) is called for:

> If giving money to the church could be reinterpreted as an expression of grace and forgiveness, it might mitigate the legalism and

moralism that sometimes characterize and curse the discussion of money in the life of the church.[6]

## The Research Design

These critiques were published well after I conceived and began the research for this book. They only serve to convince me that a field study of what I call "stewardship churches" is long overdue, for while stewardship literature is abundant, seldom have congregational stewardship programs been the subject of systematic study. And until such a study is conducted, we do not know how cogent—or how misconceived—is the critical chorus cited above. Nor do we know whether stewardship, as practiced, is really past its prime as a motivating force, both for giving money and for mobilizing volunteer energies, and whether it has relapsed into a moribund metaphor for urging congregations to dig deeper to support this year's budget. Responding to these questions is the purpose of this book: Let us visit stewardship churches and see. That is exactly what chapters 1 through 11 invite you, the reader, to do.

Let me first clarify the various ways in which I use the word stewardship. A "stewardship approach" is what characterizes "stewardship churches"—i.e., the theology of stewardship, elaborated below, becomes not just motivational rhetoric for annual fall fund-raising but an overall inspirational guide to the pastor and congregational leaders and members in seeking financial support and encouraging members to commit themselves to the church's mission and ministries. This approach usually takes a programmatic shape that varies from church to church, as we shall see. "Stewardship spirituality" means a prayerful emphasis upon acknowledging God's gifts, beginning with Jesus Christ himself as Saviour and Redeemer, and seeking ways to make return by a generous giving of oneself, one's resources and talents, to extend the Kingdom preached by Jesus. "Stewardship proponents" are those denominational and congregational leaders, consultants, pastors, and laypeople who advocate the centrality of a solid theology of stewardship and suggest how it may be implemented programmatically.

How did I embark on a two-year journey of research and writing about stewardship churches? I made my first acquaintance with churches adopting a stewardship approach as one of the authors of *Money Matters:*

*Personal Giving in American Churches.*[7] My three coauthors and I separately visited churches revealed by our surveys to be outstanding for a high rate of member giving. My case studies led me to a large Presbyterian (U.S.A.) church in Colorado, an Assemblies of God congregation in a southern California strip mall, and two Roman Catholic parishes, one in the Midwest, the other in the Southwest. To say I found each "impressive" is a decided understatement. Not only did these churches enjoy high per-capita and per-household financial support, but their arrays of ministries, outreach, quality of worship and liturgy, and overall enthusiasm of members would be the envy of any church, regardless of denomination. These churches found their way into our book as exemplars of vital, active, high-giving churches and of how a stewardship ideal[8] could be preached and practiced to galvanize a particular congregation. I was impressed enough to wonder (1) how such churches achieved what they did and (2) what different forms a stewardship approach might take in a wider variety of churches.

In spring 1996, I obtained a grant from the Lilly Endowment (the sponsor of our church-giving study) for a more focused study of churches that had adopted a stewardship approach to both monetary giving and to members' volunteer activity for ministry outreach. With the encouragement of Phil Williams, director of the Ecumenical Center for Stewardship Studies in Indianapolis, I asked the national finance and stewardship offices of mainline churches for the names of four congregations, including large and small, located in various areas of the United States, regarded as noteworthy for their stewardship programs. Six denominations responded with names of congregations: the Episcopal Church, the Evangelical Lutheran Church in America, the Presbyterian Church (U.S.A.), the Christian Church (Disciples of Christ), the American Baptist Churches, and the United Church of Christ. I received a similar list of Roman Catholic parishes from Matthew Paratore, director of the National Catholic Stewardship Council, Inc., in Washington, D.C. Aided by a sabbatical leave from the University of New Mexico in fall 1996, I was able between mid-August and mid-December to visit two local churches from each of the six mainline Protestant denominations and six Catholic parishes (subjects of a future book). I selected 11 mainline congregations for this volume, since one American Baptist congregation had no pastor when I visited and information was incomplete.

Some readers will recognize this book's affinity with congregational studies, a major research field today. Such scholars as Nancy Ammerman, Stephen Warner, Jackson Carroll, Carl Dudley, and William McKinney are among those who have put all church researchers in their debt. Carroll, Dudley, and McKinney edited the first *Handbook of Congregational Studies* in 1986.[9] Deserving of major focus, the contributors said, were a congregation's identity, context, processes, and programs. These elements have remained crucial in subsequent congregational studies. A dozen years later came an excellent successor volume edited by Ammerman, Carroll, Dudley, and McKinney.[10] Researchers were urged to give attention to dimensions emphasized in the first *Handbook* (though "context" became "ecology" and "culture" was added to "identity"), but also to theology, resources, and leadership. In any thoroughgoing study of congregations, the totality of these elements must be given attention and woven into the research design.

Let me be clear: I do not intend the church portraits you are about to read as full-blown congregational studies. That has not been my purpose. While all the dimensions cited above make an appearance from time to time, theology comes closest to the one I have chosen to emphasize. "Practical theology" would perhaps be the most appropriate term: How is the theology of stewardship expressed, enfleshed, played out in this church? Time did not permit anything like an ethnographic study of each church. An ethnographer not only obtains accounts from the principal people involved but also labors to discern spoken and unspoken meanings, interactions and reactions, gathering official and unofficial versions from a wider variety of sources. Such an approach takes time and has the potential, of course, for a more textured portrait than I was able to draw, though now and then I was let in on aspects of "the other side of the story." All in all, however, I believe that the information and insights I drew from my interviews and observations sufficed to identify the main contours of each church's stewardship orientation; that is, how a stewardship approach made a difference within this congregation and how that difference is manifested.

At the outset of my research, I developed a set of survey questions (see appendix) to probe how a church came to adopt its stewardship approach and how it was working in various aspects of congregational life. My first interview, of course, was with the pastor. The next was usually with the chair—and sometimes the members—of the finance or stewardship committee and the chair and members of the church governing body (vestry, session, etc.), then with the associate pastor and others recommended by the pastor or by one of those interviewed. I made it a point to talk to secretaries and receptionists, since they are often the best informed about daily goings-on in the church (now and then I would hear that "other side of the story"!). At times I was invited to sit in on committee meetings—always an enlightening experience. The pastor sometimes suggested lunch or dinner for a second conversation. On several visits, I was invited to stay in the parsonage or rectory, an ideal setting for further conversation. I asked for and was always provided with a yearly financial report and other documents relevant to the stewardship enterprise; e.g., descriptions of the church's various ministries and, occasionally, the pastor's written or taped stewardship sermons. I also managed to get in touch with most of the pastors again in late 1998 or early 1999 to obtain updates of the information provided two years earlier. In one case (First Presbyterian, Fort Worth), most of the information was gathered in late 1998.

Transcribed taped interviews thus became *accounts* by "principal actors" of each church. The most "official" tended to be those by the pastor and the finance and stewardship chairs. Less official accounts were voiced by committee members after a meeting and by ordinary church members during informal conversations after Sunday worship service. Enthusiasm about their church was what I usually heard. Once in a while, someone felt free to raise concerns or register disagreement with what was going on or what was being planned. Overall, I believe that for the most part, my informants provided a reasonably clear, coherent, and balanced picture of how stewardship was working in their church, and that is what I try to present. That being the case, what is my general sense of the theological meaning of stewardship as it emerges in the "church stories" to follow?

## The Theology of Stewardship

The good steward who took responsible care of the estate that was entrusted to him is a familiar figure to Bible readers: The master departs on a trip, and the steward is left in charge. The master will ask for an accounting when he returns. "What have you done with what I entrusted to you?" The main idea, of course, is that all of creation is a gift to human beings. More specifically, each of us is entrusted with the particular set of created gifts and good things we have been given in this life. Each of us is responsible for how these gifts are used; we will someday have to give our own account. The stewardship ideal urges each Christian disciple to acknowledge what he or she has received by being ready to return these gifts to God through

Jesus Christ. Return is expressed in willingness to use one's time, talent, and treasure to advance the Kingdom of God as expressed in the mission of the church to which the believer belongs.

The notion of sacrifice frequently accompanies stewardship exhortations: One's time for volunteering is valuable (ask "the overworked American"); so, in another sense, are one's talents—no one is justified in assuming that he or she has no talent that can benefit the community. Each person does. Finally, one's treasure or financial assets is to be given generously. As we shall see, tithing is sometimes held up as an ideal or, short of the full tithe, some form of proportional giving. Giving one's "first fruits" to the church is often invoked; as one stewardship chair put it, "If you're into stewardship, when the salary check arrives, it's automatic. The top 10 percent, or whatever proportion you can generously afford, is set aside. After *that* you can start paying your bills."

Stewardship authors and proponents are quick to emphasize the spiritual underpinnings of stewardship. To a person, they deplore any notion that stewardship is synonymous with fund drives and direct solicitations of money or pledges. This assumption is considered a harmful distortion, for it detracts from the primacy to be accorded God's sovereignty over *all* gifts we have received, not just money and possessions. The spirituality of stewardship has been elaborated at length, yet experienced and successful stewardship pastors unanimously caution that getting across this ideal to a congregation takes time (more than one pastor spoke of "four or five years"). As one remarked to me, "Stewardship is no gimmick. It is deeply challenging to everyone, myself included. You're asking your people to pray and think about God's primacy over their check registers and over their daily schedules. You can't hit any closer to home than that. And the first thing they're going to do is look at their pastor and see if he's practicing what he preaches."

A stewardship approach, as this book will illustrate, really begins a kind of dialogue between pastor and congregation over some of the most sensitive terrain in his or her life and theirs. It will become clear in these pages that stewardship spirituality and what it asks of pastor and people are profoundly countercultural. It is precisely for this reason that churches adopting this approach vary in depth of commitment to stewardship, in how it is presented and pursued, and in how church members react to it. Its countercultural character also helps to explain why it takes years before stewardship ideals begin to take effect and make a notable difference in the life of a church—a consideration leading us directly to congregational leadership.

## Pastoral Leadership

Early on in my church visits, it became evident that the pastor's leadership was a linchpin of stewardship endeavor. Pastoral enthusiasm, persistence, and encouragement were quintessential to the success of stewardship in the church. Yet I knew I had not named the essence of the leadership quality that characterized every single pastor, regardless of denomination. It simply eluded me. Shortly after I had completed my visits, I came across management expert Peter Block's book *Stewardship: Choosing Service over Self-Interest*. His opening chapter is titled "Replacing Leadership with Stewardship." The following quotation emphasizes the very quality I encountered (though it varied by degrees) in every pastor with whom I spoke. I first thought of it as "being comfortable delegating," but it is much more than that:

> In its commitment to service, stewardship forces us then to yield on our desire to use good parenting as a basic form of governance. We already know how to be good parents at work. The alternative, partnership, is something we are just learning about. Our difficulty with creating partnerships is that parenting—and its stronger cousin, patriarchy—is so deeply ingrained in our muscle memory and armature that we don't even realize we are doing it.[11]

These pastors refused to parent their congregations. They understood Block's further elaboration that "dependency is the collusion required for patriarchy and parenting to endure."[12] In preaching and teaching and challenging about stewardship, pastors tried to make it clear that they were inviting parishioners to claim their own autonomy where time, talent, and treasure were concerned—the decision-making was truly theirs. Neither pastor nor stewardship committee nor anyone else was sitting in judgment on them. These pastors were aware, once more in Block's words, that

> setting goals for people, defining the measure of progress toward these goals, and then rewarding them for reaching them does not honor their capabilities . . . stewardship asks us to serve our organizations and be accountable to them without caretaking and without taking control. And in letting caretaking and control go, we

hold on to the spiritual meaning of stewardship: to honor what has been given to us, to use power with a sense of grace, and to pursue purposes that transcend short-term self-interest.[13]

No implication should be drawn that these pastors failed to be leaders in exhorting their parishioners, in suggesting avenues of ministry, or in asking for accountability from staff and committee or board chairs. These things they certainly did. But I'm not sure a phrase like "open leadership style" is adequate either. Such a characterization fails to do justice to the depth of their belief that stewardship is an *invitation* to share, to give back and to sacrifice and to grow through this experience toward a total trust in God as one gives back to God. After all, as one pastor succinctly put it, "this is *their* church; it isn't *my* church." They knew, of course, that some of their church members would respond generously, others so-so, many hardly at all. Some would hear only "money" and be upset. All these were risks to be taken in an effort to empower church members to forsake passivity and dependence and become *intentional* (a concept I shall return to) about their decisions concerning ministry and the allotment of their time and money.

Among the pastors' aims, of course, was to "flatten out the 80-20 principle," as one put it—a common pattern of a small minority doing most of the work and the giving. What makes this stance difficult to come by, of course, is the notion, taken for granted since seminary days, that I, the pastor, am solely responsible for growth in revenues, ministries, congregational morale, and other criteria of success. The notion is not easily assimilated that pastoral responsibility means facilitating church members' own growth in awareness of and responsiveness to God's gifts and that *from* this growth the congregation will manifest the success criteria. Such is the case particularly when the process takes time. Once this perspective dawned on me, I could understand why so few pastors fully adopt the stewardship approach: It truly runs contrary to embedded, conventional notions and rhetoric of pastoral responsibility. Block has it right: Patriarchy indeed means that "vision, direction and leadership are expected to come from the top."[14] Looked at this way, putting a stewardship approach into play is indeed nothing less than revolutionary from the bottom up. These pastors knew that and were willing to run the risks.

## Some Cautionary Notes

I hasten to add that none of the churches portrayed in these pages is a perfect stewardship model. Some churches new to a stewardship approach struggled to get it going. For example, while most of the pastors urged some form of pledging or tithing, none succeeded in getting every member or household to do so (most would say such a goal is unrealistic in any case). Volunteers were sometimes in short supply. I heard occasional grumbles from church members about one or another aspect of a program.

Let me go a few steps further: I do not maintain that a stewardship approach is the *only* path to building an admirably dynamic church. Consultants continue to write books and conduct workshops prescribing five steps or ten steps toward creating a successful church. While acknowledging stewardship as a helpful theme, these authors do not necessarily give it a central position. But when a church under firm, consistent, and enthusiastic pastoral leadership that involves open consultation with church staff and members adopts a stewardship approach, that choice carries with it a deeply troubling message going way beyond "steps toward success." The very meaning of money, wealth, one's time priorities–all of which we come to regard in our culture as highly personal possessions–is profoundly challenged. Gospel warnings about the spiritual dangers of hoarding and hanging onto and being "busy Marthas" assume new life. What we do with our money and our time moves from periphery to center. Pastors and lay witnesses lead by behavioral example and by taking the risk of annoying, even alienating, some church members as they make explicit a truly countercultural message of the Gospels. I return to this motif not just because pastors nodded vigorously when I mentioned it, but because they were explicitly conscious that our consumer culture truly bids us at every turn to spend or invest or save up (or all three!). Nothing, to say the least, in advertising or consumer tips or advice suggests spiritual danger in making "things" central in our lives. That is the task of pastoral leadership, one taken seriously by the voices you will hear.

Adopting a stewardship approach, then, is not just a choice of one among many techniques. It holds the promise of being truly transformative of individuals and communities along a path of calling and of discipleship. The outcome, pastors affirmed, was freedom arising from returning generously to God what has been entrusted to us in forms of time and talent and money. Nothing easy here, as will be apparent in these narratives of struggle, hopefulness, and (at times) success.

A point, however: In no way do I want "success" to convey a primacy to financial support. Stewardship success is *not* to be equated with large revenues; in some of the churches, you will observe that revenues are not particularly impressive. So in each account, while noting revenues and congregational size, I do not highlight them in charts and tables. I deliberately incorporate these data into the narrative itself as but one element in this church's stewardship striving. That, I think, is as it should be.

## Points of Comparison

Finally, keep in mind that I am presenting churches from denominations commonly diagnosed as "ailing." The condition of the patients is well publicized, and prescriptions abound. The main symptom, of course, has been a membership decline that became apparent by the mid-1960s. Hardest hit were "liberal" denominations such as the Episcopal Church, the United Church of Christ, and the Presbyterian Church (U.S.A.). Less afflicted were "moderate" denominations like the United Methodist Church, the Evangelical Lutheran Church in America, the Christian Church (Disciples of Christ), and the Reformed Church in America. Big gainers, on the other hand, were Holiness, Pentecostal, and more recently, evangelical churches. Of course, it is sometimes forgotten (or at least less often noted) that individual congregations within both liberal and moderate families have thrived, are thriving today, and simply do not fit the mold of declining churches. The "liberal" and "moderate" congregations I portray in this book are pretty good examples. "Not us" was the reaction when I sketched the more pessimistic portrayal for a pastor or finance committee or congregation members over doughnuts and coffee. Or: "Sounds like the church I [or we] came from." You will hear many such voices in these pages.

Finally, in my concluding reflections on each church, I refer to some observations about church growth set down by C. Kirk Hadaway and David A. Roozen in *Rerouting the Mainstream*, one of the best (and most hopeful) books I know on mainline churches. These points are distilled from their chapter 3, "The Congregation: When Radical Change is Required."[15] While not all growing churches have adopted a stewardship approach, the ones in this volume share many if not all the traits of growing congregations, together with some of their own, as I shall elaborate.

1. Continued growth requires lasting change in the *identity*, *vision*, and *direction* of the church if growth is to endure beyond initial enthusiasm arising from a campaign or program.

2. Growing churches seem friendlier and more welcoming to visitors, reflecting their strong sense of purpose. The church emanates a sense of mission and of lives being changed, creating a compelling sense of value to be found here.

3. Evangelistic outreach is strongly visible. Hadaway and Roozen regard this emphasis as the single most important action related to growth.

4. Worship services carry a sense of excitement and expectancy closely related to the energies propelling evangelistic outreach.

5. Pastors and pastoral staffs are or become people of faith and are willing to work with lay leaders, staff, and church members to rethink the identity and purpose of the church.

6. Evangelical churches need not be looked to as models for growth. Solutions are at hand within mainstream congregations themselves.

7. The factors cited above are much more important to a local church's identity and vitality than whether it is theologically liberal or conservative.

## A Personal Word

I am a practicing Roman Catholic. Prior to this research, I seldom walked into a Protestant church—and then usually to attend a wedding or a funeral. As I found a seat at Sunday worship services in an American Baptist or Lutheran or Disciples congregation, I sometimes pictured the Irish pastors I remembered from parochial school years rolling in their graves! The truth is that I gained a heartfelt appreciation for the spiritual richness of each tradition, novice though I was. I often felt uplifted by beautiful services enhanced by well-directed choirs and inspired by wonderful sermons. Sometimes matters of Scripture and theology found their way into my conversations with pastors, much to my enlightenment. On many a plane flight home, I found myself reflecting on what I had experienced and thanking God for opening doors into churches whose everyday lives I knew so little about. Why, I wondered, had I not opened these doors earlier? Quick and ready answers abound, I suppose, but I believe deeper ones remain to be pondered and prayed about.

CHAPTER 1

# COMBINING TOLERANCE
# WITH A VERY CLEAR FOCUS
*Acton Congregational Church, Acton, Massachusetts*

Write an "I" into the name of this historic New England town of 18,000 citizens, and you get "action." This word play begins, at least, to convey the dynamism of one 850-member church. Cynthia Williams, coordinator of lay programs, is quick to say why the congregation attracts young families, grafting them onto the core of older parishioners who still make up 40 percent of Acton Congregational Church (ACC):

> What they [young families] find here on their first visit is what brings them back, and that is a very welcoming sense, a combination of the joyousness of being a member of the Christian faith, and yet a vigorous sense of "We are at work here." I think it appeals to people to have expectations made of them. The Sunday school, of course, is a very, very good program, and most of our new people are young families looking for the right kind of program for their child. That brings them back for a second visit. Also, though, what they hear from the pulpit is good food for thought. It's intriguing, it's edifying, and that is part of the magic taking place at our worship services.

A male member notes that the wide variety of programs the church sponsors means that "there are a lot of different ways for people to belong to this church." But programs aren't the whole story by themselves:

> I think it's the openness, the welcomeness of the church, together with programs that allow people to participate in ways they can and want to–all have been very powerful in helping this church grow.

Stewardship at Acton, the member continues, is a reciprocal process that evokes strong loyalties among members.

> I know that I give because this church gives so much to me. It's my lifeline, and if I didn't have this church personally, I would not be the person I am today, or feel the strength that I do; I would not feel the love for Christ that I feel today. So for me it's a giving back of what I've been given because I feel so blessed by the people of this church.

For Ann Thayer, chair of the canvass committee (1996), educational opportunities were part of what drew her and her husband to ACC:

> The preaching here is great. That draws a number of people. Nine years ago, when my husband and I were looking for a church—we had no children at the time—we wanted one with adult-education opportunities where we ourselves could contribute as well as be fed, and that was clearly available here. Then there's the strength of the music program [that] many find attractive. The spiritual life here is very vibrant. People who want that without some of the baggage they may have had in another denomination—particularly the Catholic Church—are drawn here. You know, they don't want to be alienated from God, but they don't mind leaving that institution.

These comments reflect a healthy, growing, youthful congregation. Of the 337 households in ACC, 55 percent have children under 18, 28 percent are couples with adult children or no children, and 17 percent are single people. The concluding summary from the 1996 status report, "Sustaining Our Mission," exhibits with justifiable pride the "upside" of a church that runs counter to the depressing trends in community and denomination:

> No wonder we feel the excitement and stress of change in our congregation. Almost half of our currently served membership has joined since 1990. Average Sunday School attendance has grown 23 percent in two years. We've experienced change in worship frequency and times. Our staff has grown substantially.

We are a vibrant community in a time of decline of Christian commitment in our communities. The Acton Congregational Church has grown to the point of being the seventh largest in the Massachusetts Conference of the UCC [United Church of Christ]–a conference whose membership has fallen 50 percent in the last 25 years.

## Pastoral Leadership

Praise for the preaching implies a respected pastor. The Rev. Richard Olmsted arrived in 1983 with an understanding from the congregation that his principal calling was to preach. That he has been eminently successful was echoed by all members with whom I spoke: "Don't leave without hearing Dick preach." With a doctorate from Yale Divinity School, Dick Olmsted is well-prepared to reach an educated congregation that includes Harvard and MIT faculty members. He had come to a church already active but added a new dimension:

> I think, if anything, I tried to give a theological focus about activity, and that included fund-raising and that sort of thing–a theological focus to the church's life. This is a quite orthodox Christian church, rooted in the Reformation. I can happily relate to Lutherans and Presbyterians who come, and to Roman Catholics, too. They find here something they recognize as Christian faith and not something wildly different. Continuing and heightening the Christ-centered focus was something the congregation was looking for when they called me, and that's what I've worked hard on.
>
> The most important thing in the life of the church, I believe, is its worship life. That's the center of the church's life. That's why people come here, I believe, and they find all kinds of interests and enthusiasms that involve them in its life, including ministering to one another and ministering outside of this fellowship. We have wonderful music you'll hear on Sunday. You get people coming through our doors for various reasons initially, like their children, and feeling somewhat guilty about neglecting their religious education. Later they tell me over and over, "I came at first for my children, but now I come for myself." That's because the vertical relationship to God has become very important to them.

Olmsted spoke of the "Confessing Christ Movement" in the United Church of Christ. "I am on the national board of that and an active participant in it. It's a movement that works against the grain of a lot of what happens in the UCC."

"Doing theology," he remarked, is not what has usually led people into the UCC. Other agendas have prevailed. "Theology tends to get tacked onto those agendas." The confessing movement, then, involves a fundamental shift of priorities:

> Just like I think worship is the heart of the life of Acton Congregational Church, so I think theology should be the heart and the life of a denomination. I don't think it is now in the UCC. We are very unclear theologically as a denomination: [the] UCC has suffered, I believe, from being at the all-inclusive end of the spectrum where tolerance is everything. This church, as I try to tell people when they join it, combines tolerance with a very clear focus. We are all trying to grow in one direction, into deeper discipleship to Jesus Christ, and we are very clear about that. There are a lot of churches that are very clear about where they are going but not very tolerant about where people are; other churches are very tolerant about where people are and have no idea where they are going. This church combines both of those things together, and I think that is part of its unique genius.

## Stewardship Emphasis

Dick Olmsted formed an "ad hoc stewardship committee" during his first year. The church had known little emphasis on stewardship, but Olmsted saw things differently:

> I thought, this is a wealthy community. I believed it was very important that people share out of what they have received. I want the church to provide people with all kinds of hands-on opportunities for serving others and caring for one another in the church. We have very extensive ways in which that is possible here. These became emphases that I think made a big difference in the sharing of resources also. When I first came here, conditions were crowded.

The church needed to build a new sanctuary, so I worked to get that started my first year. All these things made a difference in terms of people sensing that church life and churchmanship, you might say, demanded more of them than I think they had generally been aware of before.

A rocky ride often characterizes the beginning of stewardship emphases. The Acton church was no exception. My conversations with church members brought out what Olmsted described as a pivotal stewardship experience. Following a big capital-fund drive in the mid-1980s, pledging for the budget that year was flat, not an unusual experience in any church.

A couple of years later we just realized we couldn't live with the situation. We then called in a UCC fund-raiser who did a kind of challenge campaign where people were visited in their homes and challenged on the basis of what they give and what it seems they might be able to give ... to see if they couldn't raise their pledge by so much and so on. Well, a lot of people, as you can imagine, especially here in New England, were just up in arms about this. They just hated it and became very angry.

Members who canvassed door to door that year under this approach indeed walked into withering receptions when, under instruction, they "got up-close and personal" about the member's finances. As one woman remarked, "I don't know how they knew the size of my mortgage and how many kids I had in college at the time." Reactions from both canvassers and canvassed amounted to "Let's never do this again." One canvasser protested, "They jumped on me about how dare I do this and call on [them] this way, and I thought, whoa!"

The outcome was adoption in 1993 of "Faith-Promise,"[1] a stewardship strategy worked out by a pastor and a member of the Congregational Church of Laconia, N.H., and made available in written form for other UCC churches. As Dick Olmsted put it, "This is one where the heart of it is pledging in church, which I had always done." The distinctive note of Faith-Promise or Faith Pledging is a split between the donor's name and the donor's pledge. Olmsted explains,

Now there are two receptacles on pledge Sunday. In one of them you place a card with your name on it indicating that you have pledged, period. In the other you put the amount of your pledge only, and that is anonymous. Only you and God know who made that pledge. The whole focus is on your relationship with God in doing this. Faith pledging is the absolute opposite of someone going into your home and saying, "We'd like you to consider giving such-and-such."

*But does this really work? Doesn't it leave a lot of room for fudging?*

Not really. The remarkable thing is that we never discount pledges in figuring out our budget for the year. We don't because we've never come up short through faith pledging.

Under this method, then, everyone receives an accounting from the church financial secretary of what they have actually given, but no one except the donor knows whether that amount matches the pledge. Herein lies the "faith element." Becky is typical of many church members in her approval of Faith Pledging and where it can lead:

It's a personal thing. Nobody knows how much I pledge. Nobody is at my door telling me how much. It's up to my husband and me to make our commitment to the church. It's within *us*, our prayers. It does not come from another human being sitting in my living room making recommendations.

The other thing I think really affects my pledge amount is my involvement with the church. Now if I wasn't pulled in (and I wanted to be), I wouldn't have understood as much as I do and might have thought a smaller pledge was perfectly adequate.

## Mission Outreach

Every other year a separate drive is undertaken on behalf of missions and outreach, as distinct from local ministries. The mission and outreach program doesn't "funnel" through the denomination (UCC). "We give the denomination some money, but our own missions program gets a much larger sum. We have people who travel all over the world and bring us back suggestions for places to which we might give." A missions committee reviews these suggestions and makes recommendations for the church to support. Income pledged for the two years 1996 and 1997 ($109,432) represented a 25 percent increase over pledge income for 1994 and 1995.

The approximately 30 missions supported, besides the UCC Wider Mission (programs such as emergency aid to disaster victims, agriculture and economic development, health and welfare services, general education, and support of denominational offices and staff), represent a broad variety, e.g., Habit for Humanity Northeast, Partners with Haiti, CROP Walk, Lazarus House (serving the homeless), Teen Challenge New England, and Rosie's Place ("advocacy and support for women facing issues of racism, classism, power structures, and, most importantly, to reclaim control of their lives").

As Olmsted pointed out, many church members travel outside the United States. They frequently return with suggestions for mission projects to be supported overseas.

## Fiscal Success

Faith-Promise has yielded pledging on the part of 85 percent of the approximately 312 households currently active in the church, a level achieved by few churches anywhere. Most astoundingly, according to the "Sustaining Our Mission" status report, "100 percent of new members in the last several years have pledged." Stewardship committee members attribute this high percentage in no small way to the anonymity of Faith-Promise, which "probably has more powerful symbolism than anything else, driving home the message that giving to the church is really making a promise to God, not to an organization." In concrete terms, the approximately $484,000 pledged in 1996 toward local ministries (not including biannual pledges for ministries and outreach) amounted to over $1,500 per pledging unit, impressive by any standard.

## Preaching Stewardship

Dick Olmsted thought carefully when I asked him about "a favorite stewardship theme you like to preach on."

I certainly want to root it in the fact that God wants to give to us . . . and that it is only by opening our lives up to him that he is able to do that. One of the ways we open up is, stop worshipping money. Giving what our culture teaches us to hoard is one of the ways that we open our lives to God. But it's always a challenge to think of new ways to talk about this that will touch people's lives. Once I talked about when I was single and I didn't really belong to a church. Yet I gave every Sunday out of what I happened to have, and I would write out a check and feel good about it. But when I added up the checks at the end of the year, comparing donations to my overall salary, I realized that I was just tipping God. I was offering a token to the world's needs. So you try to remind people that there are spiritual and practical disciplines that are important to their own spiritual lives, what they need to be doing to grow in the spiritual life. This is definitely a focus of my preaching.

*The current views about liberal mainline churches would say a UCC church can't generate the kind of theology that binds people to a stewardship commitment of time, talent, and resources. This doesn't sound like your church, though.*

Well, that may be true. This is not an evangelical church. Evangelicalism seems to me Pelagian: It tends to suggest that there are things you have to do to earn your way with God. I suppose that's one of the reasons heavy demands get met in that context, but that is not the approach we have at all.

We live out of the grace of God. My approach is not to say you are damned if you don't do this; not at all. This is, as I have said, an orthodox Protestant Christian church, a Reformation-type church. It is riskier than telling people, you have got to give 10 percent, you can't be a part of this church if you don't give that much. That is not what we do. The focus is on living out of grace, not the law. The understanding of the law I try to give is of law as permission. You may become the kind of person who is open to God in this way. You commit yourself to another for life in marriage. It is not a must, it's a "may."

You are entering into the freedom of the Gospel when you obey the law of God. The law of God is gracious, rooted in the

Gospel rather than in having to prove yourself. You are not earning merits before him, you are in fact entering more deeply into your life with him, into that fellowship which is perfect freedom, living out of God's grace.

## Membership and Services

Dick Olmsted takes considerable satisfaction in the effort his staff makes to obtain accurate membership and attendance estimates.

> As a matter of fact, the ratio of people who attend church relative to our overall membership is the highest rating of any UCC church in this state. We have by far the best ratio—more than half of our membership is in church every Sunday.

New members are asked to pledge not only money but also involvement—the time-and-talent aspect of stewardship. "Worship Plus Two: A Guideline for New Members" is explicit: "[M]ake a commitment to attend worship whenever possible." But expectations don't stop there:

> Beyond that, we ask that you endeavor to become involved in at least two activities here at ACC during your first year as a new member: one activity that is for *you* (a fellowship group, Bible Study, Mother's Day Out) and one activity that is in service to *others* (Rosie's Pllace, teaching, hosting Coffee Hour, perhaps). That's "Worship plus two"!

As the church grows in membership, space becomes problematic. Olmsted mentioned an article in *The Christian Century* about declining mainline church participation. "You know, I didn't say it directly, but I hoped when I mentioned it in a sermon that it was obvious to them: 'Our church is a complete exception to this trend. We are growing; we have growing pains.' " The church's new sanctuary, built in the late 1980s, was designed to accommodate all members at one service rather than two, as the congregation was forced to do in the old building. Despite the larger worship space, however, the pressures from membership growth prompted a recent return to two services. The Sunday before I arrived (October

1996), there were exactly 271 people at each service, a figure that amazed Dick Olmsted (the total number of 542 nearly equals the estimated number of 600 regularly active members given me by Cynthia Williams).

## Volunteering for Ministries

Praise was given to the work of Cynthia Williams as coordinator of lay programs, especially the efforts of her nominating committee to assess talents and strengths of volunteers. The committee is sensitive to husbands and wives who are both in the paid labor force. "We make sure they are not asked to be on committees at the same time." Prior to my arrival, Williams had undertaken an assessment of volunteers from 1990 through 1996.

> You sometimes hear, well, the same 40 people do everything around here. I really believed the commitment was much broader, and I wanted statistics to back that up. I found that during that seven-year period, we had 271 different individuals serve on the standing committees of the church, the vast majority for three-year terms. Considering we have a core of about 600 actively engaged adult members at Acton, 271 is certainly pretty good. And that doesn't even begin to talk about Sunday school teaching, because I didn't look at those figures at all—just those serving on the board of deacons, board of trustees, Christian education committee, and so on. Only 22 were repeat performers rolling from committee to committee over seven years. I think it all reflects the fact that when people go through our new-member class, they find out that being a member is not just worshipping here, but finding a way to serve, a way to do God's work. We are very explicit here.

New members fill out an interest survey, which is reviewed in detail during their classes. But this session has been preceded by a Bible study on stewardship of time and talent. For some, it is their first experience with Bible study, and in the process the study illustrates biblical grounding for stewardship of time and talent. Names and interests are entered into a database. Activity coordinators working with Cynthia Williams phone the new members to see about placing them within church ministries.

> We have a lot of eager beavers, to tell you the truth. They don't sit back and complain about not being called. Many would let me

know if they were not called. A big part of my job is to be sensitive to whether a person has a big chunk of time or whether they are very busy people and maybe they could do one job this fall for the church. There are always a handful of people that I'm sure I'll get a "no" from. They are on the periphery, and I have decided that's OK. There will always be people who aren't joiners, their needs are different, and maybe we have to be meeting *their* needs rather than they meeting *our* needs.

Williams reflected on the broader picture of belonging to this church. She noted the sense, present in vital churches, that all are working toward being better disciples of Christ.

But we are not told exactly how to do that. We are given opportunities to learn how to do that and to grow in the faith, but we are not told programmatically how one behaves. Somehow, achieving that balance is what makes this place one where people of many different backgrounds and people who are on a lot of different points in their journeys can come together and worship in a corporate sense and be comfortable with that.

*You do have programs directed at parents and youngsters, correct?*

Yes. We offer a PEPS program about once every two years, "Parents Encouraging Parents." We also have a play group bringing together women of this church [who are at] home during the day with their children. We also do a "Mother's Day Out" from time to time. And this fall, on the other end of the spectrum, our adult education committee is offering a class Sunday evenings on caring for elderly parents—the first time we have done this.

Like many congregations undergoing a growth cycle, Acton Church members fear the loss of intimacy if the congregation keeps expanding. A few years ago, Williams remarks, she knew everyone in the church. Growth is good; everyone would have to acknowledge this. Yet she is thoughtful about intimacy and how to preserve it. Anyone in her position, she believes, is going to have to develop small-group ministries so that the intimacy will be there, even if people can't possibly know even 50 percent of the congregation personally.

Intentionally, I think, we have to move into small-group-type ministry. You know, I think there is a locus in people's minds when they reach a really high level of involvement, a point where they feel they just belong and know everybody. That's not literally true, but they know enough people to feel this is their family. I want to know as ministry coordinator what that point of involvement is. When does it arrive for people? And how can we make sure that that feeling continues?

*What forms would such groups take?*

Nothing that striking. Bible study is one way. For another set of people it might be a book-reading group, a novel-reading group, a theater group. Those may sound a little secular, but I don't think fellowship among Christians who belong to the same church would ever be a bad thing—unless it were the only thing we offered.

A new venture is a "supper club"—members sign up to attend dinner three or four times a year with others assigned. Formation of friendships is the intended outcome. The following year, as the plan proposes, "we will shuffle the deck and start new groups. They might turn out to be gourmet clubs or ethnic-cuisine clubs. But sharing meals is just an inevitable yeast to the fellowship process."

Merrill Noble, president of the Service League, waxes enthusiastic about the organization. Each fall the women who constitute the league organize an antique show that brings in $7,000 or $8,000 in two days. A large portion of the proceeds goes for beautification or needed renovations in the church. "We gave the rug in the narthex last year and were able to help with renovating the church office." The members recently took a leaf from a thriving men's organization in the church:

To build fellowship within the league, we copied the men's fellowship breakfast, which they have monthly. They have a program and a speaker. At our very first breakfast, we had 49 women come. In past years when we had occasional breakfasts, maybe 19 to 20 would show up. We do what the men do—have a core of people who call all the women of the church to ask them if they would like to come. The same caller calls the same women the next time. The men have done this, and it is very effective.

Noble sees the league as "revitalized and energized." Forty or 50 women sign up to go to Vermont for three days of spiritual renewal; a family carol-sing takes place in December; the league sponsors a child in Brazil. "So it's a growing organization. It's changing with the times, and we are very excited." Like Cynthia Williams, Merrill Noble is thoughtfully reflective:

> We can't make everyone happy, but through all the different pro-grams of the church, I think people are able to find a niche where they can make friends and where they feel like they can belong, where they can share their Christian joys, frustrations. In my pub-licity, I try to get the point across to women of our church that when we volunteer our time, we are doing it for Christ–part of our Christian duty–and to do it joyfully and cheerfully.

Personal spiritual enrichment is available through groups such as "Faith Sharing" for women. Fifteen to 20 women come weekly on Thursday morn-ings. Themes vary–e.g., identifying your spiritual gifts and talents. "It's a wonderful support group, praying for others, a great place of learning." Resembling altar calls in more evangelical churches is "Prayer After Wor-ship." About 30 members make up a group from which two people are available after each of the Sunday services to pray confidentially with anyone in the congregation who comes.

Together with men's retreats and programs on learning to pray, this church appears to provide strongly for individual and family growth in spiri-tual well-being.

## Reflection: A Scene Set for Generous Giving

Stewardship of time, talent, and treasure in a church like ACC virtually defines the entire ethos of the church and the commitments it asks of members. Here, stewardship truly bestows identity, vision, and direction. This is a church that knows what it is about and sets expectations ("strict" in this sense) yet embodies the broader traditions of tolerance and open-ness, of which the UCC is justly proud. It occurred to me too, that ACC's strong community spirit partially reflects the homogeneous (in this case, almost exclusively white) communities of mainstream Protestant churches decades ago.

While it would be easy to say the comparative affluence of the congregation accounts for strong giving and volunteering, explaining its success is not that simple. Several factors combined in the 1990s to propel this church into its present pattern of growth. A strong tradition of volunteering and service to town and larger world has deep roots in this church. As the Massachusetts economy rebounded in the 1990s, young families, many of them from professional backgrounds, moved to Acton and sought a church that would minister to their children and offer opportunities for adult participation. ACC was well prepared to offer just these attractive features, wrapped in impressive organizational forms such as the office of coordinator of lay ministries, with its firm expectations of dual-level ministry involvement (personal growth plus outreach involvement), along with pledging to both local and worldwide church. A multiplier effect sets in as volunteers interact, often in plural ministry settings, and develop close ties with other members–the "fellowshipping" dear to the broader Protestant tradition. From these ties come the enthusiasm and creative ideas for new outreach that transforms a congregation into a vital, growing, satisfying community for a majority of its members.

But ACC was blessed with another dynamic–strong leadership-that went beyond the usual profile of the eloquent and energetic pastor with a strong sense of where he wants to take the congregation. Pastor Richard Olmsted, called primarily to preach, brought with him a theological vision that invited members to a firm, biblically based commitment to the person of Jesus Christ. This vision became translated into spiritual-growth ministries too often associated almost exclusively with evangelical churches, but Olmsted took no such churches as the model for ACC. Nonjudgmental and losing none of the tolerance that is a hallmark of the United Church of Christ, Richard Olmsted also articulated challenging reflections that grounded his stewardship vision squarely in gospel cautions about the danger of riches and of easy cultural alignment with notions of possessions as "just mine" or "ours." Once his vision was accompanied by the strategy of Faith-Promise, which defined financial decision-making as a strictly private affair (comfortable to most Americans), the scene was set for growth in generous giving outlined above, marking Acton Congregational as truly exceptional.

## CHAPTER 2

# What People Give Indicates Their Spiritual Health

*St. Paul United Church of Christ, Columbia, Illinois*

Located in the middle of a small town of 7,200, St. Paul United Church of Christ celebrated its 150th anniversary in 1998. The pastor, the Rev. Robert Page, struck me as one of a kind. Few matched his forthright way of connecting spiritual well-being with money. As in every interview, I noted that some pastors prefer not to know the identities of their major givers. After all, doesn't this knowledge open the door to cozy relationships, to the appearance of being in donors' hip pockets? Page protested:

> Oh, I'm the extreme opposite. A minister who doesn't know what his people are giving is not doing his or her job. You already know what people make. We Americans guess all the time what our neighbors make, and we're good at it, so don't pretend that ministers don't do that. I look at my families in this church. I know who is a vice-president of an insurance agency; I know who owns the major excavating firm in town; I know who's a major contractor, who is teaching school, who's a nurse. I also know that the local school system ten miles down the road pays a 20-year teacher $55,000 a year. I have a couple–he's a long-term teacher and she's a night shift nurse–their combined income is $105,000. That's a no-brainer.
>
> Now, the next question is, if I know that they are giving $5,000 a year, I know their spiritual health is fairly decent. It's not up to tithing, it's not where I would like it to be, but I know at least they have a fairly healthy situation. But if I go in and look at my records and find out that they are giving only $250 a year, I know they have major spiritual-growth problems that need to be dealt with. If they come in for counseling because they're having trouble

with their daughter, and I know they're giving $5,000 a year, I know I have to counsel them less on love and caring than I do if I know they're giving only $250. Come on, the whole notion of being in someone's hip pocket if I know all this—that's a matter of professionalism. Leave aside financial records for a moment. I look out on Sunday, and I know who's there and who's not. Professionally and ethically, do I treat the person who comes just on Palm Sunday and on Christmas differently than I treat the person who comes weekly? I have ethical problems if I do. I don't think I'm inclined to treat people unfairly based on money any more than I'm biased on the issue of how frequently they come.

Robert Page's forthright approach has not alienated the congregation in the three and a half years he has been at St. Paul. While average Sunday attendance has not risen dramatically (about 340 by 1998), revenues went up by 30 percent his first year, 15 percent his second year and 7 percent the following year. Yearly giving per household he estimates at $500 to $600 (see actual per-member giving data below). He is not satisfied with these figures. But he is pleased with the response to pledging. Asking for pledges is risky when it has not been the custom, but he insists that pastors must conquer their fear and "just do it."

It's important to recognize that often what people say they won't and can't do isn't true. In my ministry, I have taken three congregations from not pledging to pledging. In only one of them was I serving full-time. In one I was a summer interim; in another I was serving part-time while in graduate school. In all of these I was told, "They'll never pledge." I heard all the excuses against pledging. I took all three of them from there to pledging. I know it can be done. I know it isn't that hard.

If all this makes Page sound like a "money-only" pastor, it does him an injustice. His is a stewardship approach carefully thought out, taught to seminary classes, and presented at UCC conference meetings. He begins with a spiritual context:

God has given us the grace and wonder of Christ. So first and foremost, we're stewards of that. Second, we're stewards of our life. With my life [have] come the talents of which I am a steward.

How do we deal with and relate to our possessions? For Page, this is "the single major issue biblically."

> I remember reading somewhere that almost a fifth or maybe a quarter of all the verses in the Bible deal with the issue of how we act as stewards of what we possess. That's more than the Bible talks about prayer, and more than the Bible talks about faith. That intrigued me, and I began studying more in that area.
>
> After I finished my doctorate, I ended up going to a local church that had a horrendous stewardship history. A month after I arrived, it was a serious question if they could make payroll. I began talking about stewardship, confronting the issue, and within two years 65 percent of the congregation was pledging. Sure, you had the occasional person who griped, but I began to see that everything you wanted to do in a church requires funding. So stewardship was something I saw as central to the life of the church.

Tithing and "first fruits" are part of his spiritual perspective. While admitting that he has few parishioners who tithe fully, he does emphasize proportionate giving and returning "the first fruits of what you have been given by God, the best, the most wonderful ones, because that's the image of God." Like many stewardship-committed pastors, Page never loses sight of what generous giving does *for* the donors:

> There's also generosity above and beyond magnanimity, the widow who gave two mites and gave all out of joy and celebration. There's the woman who pours the $10,000 oil on Jesus' feet. There's the absolute delight, thrill, and joy that a person gets out of being incredibly generous. How generosity changes our souls! We become different people. I'll talk about how God has been so generous to us; if we want to be like God, that involves being generous ourselves out of thanksgiving for what God has done. I'll even preach that you give as an investment—that what you are investing in is your community, your church. You are investing in the betterment of the community. I will preach a sense that you become fulfilled, you become greater, your life becomes fuller out of the act of generosity. But I'm certainly not going to say that if you give $1,000, God's going to give you a Mercedes next year!

## Pastor's Own Giving

Page has struggled with his own giving. At one point in his life, he gave two and a half percent of his income, noting that the figure reflects the national average of charitable giving in the United States. At present, he "works toward a tithe," acknowledging that at pledge time, "my wife hates it every year when we have to make a decision. It's one of these things we usually have a major family discussion about." The pastor's own witness is essential, he believes, a witness made explicitly clear to the congregation. Page implies that his giving can be a challenge to others:

> I state every year exactly, in dollars and cents, what I'm doing. My congregation knows—now, they may have conveniently forgotten!—exactly what I give because it was published in the newsletter. They knew that this year my weekly pledge is $92 a week.

*That's a tithe?*

> No, it's not. I'm working *towards* a tithe. What I did, for most of my ministry, was tithe my salary. Two years ago, this church moved me from a parsonage to a housing allowance. At that point, to jump to a full tithe on my salary *and* my housing allowance would have been almost $40 a week more. So I've taken that in increments. When I first jumped to a housing allowance, our giving was at about six and a half percent. I'm at 9 percent now. I'm taking several years to get to a true tithe and I'm not sure when I'll make it—next year or the following. But it's close. And it makes me the third-largest giver in my congregation.

*This seems a powerful example to your congregation.*

> I think a pastor has to do that. I believe in that. I don't like it. I'm like everybody else—I love the privacy. I would love the anonymity. I'm aware enough of my culture that says talking about money is one of those dirty subjects you don't mention. But I don't think you can witness as a minister without saying, "This is what I give." My goal has always been to get some laypeople to do the same

thing. I have yet to get anyone to get up in my church as a layperson and say, "I give $50 a week to the church." As part of our stewardship program, lay members do witness. They'll say, "I have made a major commitment to the church, I give, and here's what it has done in my life." But they won't take that last step and say, "I give 5 percent" or 10 percent or an actual figure. I keep praying that I'm going to accomplish that one year!

## Preaching a Countercultural Message

For Page, a spirituality of commitment and of giving indeed runs counter to what is considered sensible and reasonable in our society:

> What I have found in my personal life is, as my giving has increased, my worrying about money has decreased. My income hasn't gone up, but my worrying about it diminishes. My family harmony has increased. I don't think that's accidental. Heck, I can talk about this in strictly psychological terms. If I'm starting to give away $500 a month, pragmatically my mind is clearer; I do a better job of budgeting to be able to give that amount away; hence my whole financial life works better. So I make no bones about it whenever I preach stewardship. What I'm saying is revolutionary. Jesus said you can have one God and that God is either God or it is money. You can't worship both. Now you can be rich and have a deep abiding faith. But you can't worship money and worship God. You're going to worship one or the other. One of them is going to be your master. But it's slow; it's difficult to preach, it is a constantly chipping-away type of thing to tell the good news that God is a much more faithful master than money.

*On top of this today is the advertising industry, which emphasizes all that money can buy.*

> You'd better believe it! The basic message of Christianity is that you are the most important person in creation. You are so wonderful that God wants to make you a partner, an intimate partner in creation. There is nothing that can be done to make you better

than you are. You can grow and develop, but you are the most wonderful thing in creation. The basic message of advertising is that there's something desperately wrong with you, you are lacking in some way. In order for you to be whole or happy or fulfilled, you need a deodorant, a toothpaste, or a new Lexus.

*I think of the Pepsi commercial these days, which is so blatant: "Buy Pepsi and get stuff."*

Oh, yeah. But my favorite ad of all times is the Anheuser-Busch one, "I love you, man." But then "I" go over and do something else—my love means nothing compared to go getting a beer! Love itself means nothing.

## Preaching Proportional Giving

Page acknowledges that the United Church of Christ "is not a strong giving denomination," and that a handful of families, "four or five at the most," tithe a full 10 percent in his church. "But I make no bones about holding 10 percent as the biblical minimum." The first step is to get people thinking about proportional giving.

The day I convert one person to giving proportionally, I have accomplished more than if I convinced 50 people to increase their giving by a dollar a week. Because once I have convinced them to give proportionally, I don't ever have to work on them again. As their income goes up, their giving is going to go up. Chances are it's going to be fairly easy to begin moving them from where they are now, say, 2 percent, to two and a half and then 3 percent. The big challenge for me is to get somebody to think in terms of proportional giving to start with.

*But how about those who say they're giving to so many other charities like United Way?*

Give proportionally across the board. That's fine. I don't care whether your tithe is 5 percent to the church and 5 percent to the broader community. That's 10 percent, and to me that's a wonderful tithe. My question is: Have you begun thinking about your entire charitable giving in a proportional way? And if you're thinking about your entire giving proportionally, the first place you start is, what percentage am I giving to the church? Sure, Americans are generous people as a group. My theme is, how do you make the decision on what you give? I care whether they give, whether it's to church or United Way or both. To me, generosity is the important thing. I've learned a long time ago that the individuals who give well to the church give well outside the church. The ones who give hardly anything to the church give hardly anything anywhere else.

*So they're not going to be big United Way givers either?*

I have yet to meet a person in any church that I have served who is giving humongous amounts to United Way and nothing to the church. Now I have one family in this church that is borderline poverty and gives virtually nothing to this church, but is one of the most active families I have seen in the community. They sell hot dogs and do the raffle tickets and all types of things for Blue Jay football, working hard to raise money for that program. That's the only family in my entire ministry that is generous outside the church and not inside the church. Theirs is a case of borderline poverty where their giving is entirely in time and talent and activity, and that's fine. For the most part, though, generous giving in one area is associated with generous giving across the board.

## Why Not Preach Money?

Page has worked with his UCC conference in stewardship. He thus has a wider base of experience with other pastors than is commonly found. His first observation centered on the topic of who goes into ordained ministry in the first place.

The vast majority are people who are loving, caring, warm, supportive people. If you used Myers-Briggs psychological testing, 80 percent are a feeling type of person. That is, I make decisions based on how it makes me feel and makes other people feel. You then add on top of that a basically liberal theology, which entails a wide diversity of acceptance, where we tend to preach very strongly the warmth, the love, the caring and nurturing qualities of God.

When you take it to the next step and talk commitment, and we're talking here about commitment in the most cold, hard, practical form there is—money—it really hits people where they feel it. Some people are going to get mad. You cannot talk money in the church without having somebody get mad at you. And they're getting mad at you because that gives them an excuse not to raise their pledge. But they are going to get mad. If emotionally you can't deal with conflict or you can't deal with people who are upset with you, you will find reasons not to preach money. So I think the reason the vast majority of pastors don't push stewardship in the church is that they don't want to deal with the emotional cost of advocating stewardship.

*You seem to think, though, that stewardship can be pushed in a way that doesn't engender a reaction in the congregation along the lines of "This is just another way of dunning us for money."*

No. I can't do that. The fact of the matter is, if you ask for money, there's going to be somebody out there that's going to say, "All the church ever does is talk about money." You only avoid their screaming if you never ask for money. My point is, just because someone's going to complain about it is not a reason not to do it. It's like preaching on racial harmony. I'm going to get somebody mad.

The thing is, you can't preach the Gospel without, at some point, having people get upset. Every minister I know will do some of that. My point is, the one place where they're going to get the most annoyed is money, because it hits closest to home. No matter what you say, someone's going to feel guilty because they're giving a buck a week and they know that doesn't cut it. But they expect to be praised for that buck a week, and I'm sorry, but I won't praise them. I won't condemn them, but I won't praise them for a buck a week.

*So what advice do you give pastors?*

Take a risk. Just do it. The life you live after they start pledging is so much easier than the one you lived before! I can deal with it from a pastoral viewpoint: There's major self-interest here!

## "Miracle Sundays"

Fund-raising for specific purposes is part of Page's stewardship endeavor. One particular strategy seems part and parcel of an aggressive can-do approach.

> Almost two years ago we had a Miracle Sunday. We had five tasks of delayed maintenance that just had to be faced. To do them all amounted to $44,000. I had done these Sundays in a number of churches before, so I know they work. The church was absolutely convinced it was going to fail. But we went ahead and, yes, you have to do four or five weeks' advance promotion. You plan to receive the offerings on that one Sunday, but some does dribble in later over a month or so. But however much money we get, that's how much work we're going to do. Well, the congregation almost fainted dead away when they discovered you could run a Miracle Sunday for $44,000 and end up raising $50,000 on one Sunday!

*Did this involve bazaars and casinos and that sort of thing?*

> No, no, this was pure and simply saying, we want you to give above and beyond your regular giving for this one-time special project. Now, you have to understand that we stressed the giving was not to come out of your regular checking account. We expect you to go to your savings to get the money. We even said, you might want to think about giving us stock instead of cash; we even said, think of selling a boat you haven't used in three years. The whole theme was that this was to be given out of your accumulated assets, not out of your fluid cash. This is like when you go to the doctor and you end up having to go into your savings account. This is the church asking you to do the same. Now we had five people who said, I can't give the whole amount I'd like

now, but I will give this much a month. But the vast majority came in single checks. Two of those checks were for $5,000. When I've done these Sundays before, I even wrote recommendations on the card saying, I'll do $1,000, I'll do $500, I'll do $300. If you don't suggest a gift, they're not going to give it. I always suggest a gift.

## Funds and Endowment

The St. Paul pledge card opens with a well-expressed stewardship message:

> As you give to the church and to its mission and ministry in the name of Jesus Christ, celebrate that you are growing as a steward and as a person made in the image of a giving God.

Exemplifying Rob Page's direct, lay-it-out-there approach to his congregation, the card continues, "Now in response to God's gifts, I want to grow in my faithfulness to God and in my giving to God's church and world." Then comes the expected line indicating what the person/pledging unit plans to give weekly or monthly or annually to the General Fund (regular offering). Many (perhaps most) pledge cards stop right there. Not this one:

---

I have calculated what percentage this is of my income and

_____  I am moving toward tithing
_____  I am now tithing (giving 10%)
_____  I am giving more than a tithe

This new commitment  _____  is more money than I am now giving
                     _____  is a larger % of my income than I
                             am now giving

---

There's more. Pledging at St. Paul, unlike most churches, calls for support not only of the general fund but also of "brick-and-mortar" needs:

I also plan to give $_____to the Building and Maintenance Fund
(weekly) (monthly) (annually).

Name_____(please print)

Rob Page assured me that a "vast majority" of his parishioners have no objection to this direct appeal to tithe (parishioners seemed to echo his conviction, though not entirely, as will be shown below); yet *actual* per-member giving of this congregation of 1,100 does not seem notably impressive. On the other hand, Page has had less than four years to get across not just a tithing ideal, but the very practice of pledging. I give two sets of figures, one for calendar year 1995, provided to me during my visit in August 1996, and one for calendar year 1997, mailed to me later. "Overall giving" combines general fund and building-and-maintenance pledges together with plate offerings, Lenten and Easter offerings, and "other contributions."

|      | Overall Giving | Per Member Giving |
|------|----------------|-------------------|
| **1995** | $282,940    | $257              |
| **1997** | $290,424    | $264              |

Yet financial stewardship at St. Paul goes beyond reliance on offerings. This church is blessed by a long-standing "St. Paul Endowment Fund" consisting of both government securities and common stock. By 1997 it had accumulated a principal of $595,405 and had gained that year an additional $282,426, for a total of $877,832. Overseen by the consistory (the governing body in a UCC congregation), the fund receives bequests left by estates of deceased members. Three such bequests totaling $130,000 came in 1997. An additional $33,408 from another estate was left for upkeep of building and property.

The consistory's annual report for 1997 expresses appreciation for the $25,784 interest income yielded by the fund:

We rejoice at the mission and ministry which we as a church have been able to help through the interest income of our St. Paul Endowment Fund. Through the insight of those wonderful members who gave gifts to St. Paul, the principal has been invested, allowing the income to be used for our own church and also missions and ministries throughout the wider church.

There follows a list of 14 beneficiaries, including "Christmas gifts for Hoyleton Teen Parent Program," "Gifts for families from our church experiencing difficult times," a gift to a new neighboring UCC congregation toward its mortgage, and another for "Capital Funds of Illinois South Conference" (of UCC). These gifts, the report continues, "given out of members' strong faith and love for St. Paul Church, have continued to be a living legacy to touch the lives of those in need." The very presence of the endowment, then, enables Pastor Page to remind parishioners of the possibility of leaving a bequest to the church, citing visible benefits, in a kind of "success builds on success" approach.

## Time and Talent

As two expressions of stewardship, time and talent are kept separate from finances. Page believes in "doing the money at one point in the year and time and talent in another." Just as he recognizes giving to United Way or to a Little League team as stewardship of money, so Page finds praiseworthy the gift of one's time to worthwhile causes outside of church:

> It so happens, the Sunday you're here we're honoring two members in our bulletin. One of them worked hard to get a branch post office put up. So we're acknowledging the branch which will carry his name and was dedicated this week. The other person is going to be honored for 37 years' work in the public library. This way we recognize the stewardship of service. In fact, we have an article that runs every month in our newsletter that's called "The Church Mouse." We praise those members for how they dedicate and give of themselves, whether it's community service or church service or something else.

For Page, one of the biggest challenges regarding members' time and talent is finding "significant volunteer work." People are often reluctant to engage in "make-work" and often see typical church committee agendas as just that.

> They typically say something like, "We come for two hours every month, and half the time I don't see anything we're accomplishing. I'm far more willing to spend that same amount of time down at the nursing home, visiting somebody, or fixing a dinner at a shelter. I want to see what I'm doing is making a tangible difference somewhere." It's far easier to get people to volunteer when they see direct effects.

Half the membership was born and raised in the church. In fact, three- or four-generation families are not uncommon among members. Page sees a double edge here:

> This situation is wonderful for providing networks of caring, support, [and] love when you are part of the church and in times of crisis. But if you have just moved into the community and you want to get on the inside of the power structure, the operation and ministry of this church, it takes a while for them to realize you're even here.
>
> Of course if you're vivacious and outgoing, you may be brought inside rather quickly. But if you tend to be somewhat shy or retiring, you could go ten years before people notice you're around. I sit with a nominating committee, and one of the hardest things facing me is to get somebody—even one who has been extremely active but here less than ten years—onto the consistory. I've been here four years and haven't succeeded yet! When it comes to nominating someone for that central ruling body of the church, there's the sense that we keep it in the family. Less than ten years, you're not part of that family yet!

Page believes strongly in rotating committee memberships so that church members don't feel there's a clique that keeps running the committee. Furthermore, just being on the stewardship committee is in itself an education in stewardship, and this experience should be spread around. "You can't serve two or four years on that committee without beginning to understand how stewardship relates in the whole life of the church. It's a vital experience."

Page is deeply appreciative, as are most pastors, of what volunteers accomplish. In his senior pastor's report for 1995, he reflected,

> The one thing I have learned in my ministry is that very little of what happens in a church is the work of the pastor. The real life and vitality of the church lies in the laity, the members who give so much of their time, talent, creativity, and money.

He went on to praise the musicians "who share their gifts in the vocal choirs, bell choirs, and instrumental ensembles." He concluded his report with two paragraphs that deserve full citation for demonstrating the vitality of ministry at St. Paul and how deeply the pastor appreciates it.

> One can't begin to figure how much the healing, loving, and grief work is worth that takes place during the funeral lunches made possible by the Kitchen Committee. We have a superior Church School program because of the teachers, many of whom have served longer than I've been ordained. Nor can we begin to count the value of all the maintenance done by the Property Committee and the scores of volunteers they recruit for painting, cleaning, and other work. The more than fifty adults that are taking part in the confirmation program by preparing meals, acting as sponsors, leading music and dancing, and serving on the planning committee have made our confirmation program a fantastic one.
>
> Even in the areas of missions, which we often think of only in terms of money sent elsewhere, volunteers and dedicated members are what make these programs work. There are the people who . . . record the dial-a-prayer, the members who transport people to the hospitals and doctors' offices, those who help with church services in the nursing homes, those who take home communion to shut-ins, and those who collect and transport the food and clothing for Kindercottage. Those are only our "in house" missions; we have hundreds who do the mission outreach of the church in community, county, and denominational work. We ended this year

in sound financial shape but, more importantly, we ended the year in fantastic volunteer shape. It has been a privilege to be a part of the faith and ministry of this congregation. I look forward to the future God has for us.

## The Stewardship Committee

My conversation with members of this committee underlined their sense of the committee's vital role in the congregation. One said:

> I think people don't realize what it takes to maintain a church to start with. They think others are going to pay for the heating and the cooling, keep the lights on and all of that. They think it's a gratis kind of thing. But of course it can't be. It's just like running a home. You have to pay taxes, furnish the home, etc. Same thing with the church. Someone has to foot the bills. If you believe in the church, support it.

Others pointed out how "thinking right" about the church involves going beyond just a question of whether a family should tithe or not. Instead, what can the church offer you? When you get to thinking of what the church offers, "money won't be the problem." Involvement on church boards and committees engenders just this outlook.

Available time was not a central issue for these committee members. I heard from them what I heard elsewhere: If there's something you believe in, you will find the time. "Excuses are with us to the end of time," in the words of one member, but if one truly believes in the purpose of the church, "it's not that difficult to say yes." To get started in ministries, each new member receives a pamphlet listing all church organizations. At new members' orientation, committee and board members come to talk about their service.

Committee members generally approved of the pastor's approach to proportionate giving, though with reservations. Being asked on the pledge card if one accepted the challenge to increase one's giving percentage this year, or even if one was working *toward* a tithe was fine, *as long as* one was not *required* (a) to sign the card and (b) to state whether one had *arrived* at a tithe or at some specific percentage. An elderly member further reflected on giving as a life-cycle phenomenon: When you're very young, you may get into the habit of giving because your Sunday school class regularly gives. Going to college, "you have no money at all!" Married and starting a new family? Begin giving again.

> And when you're my age, you've got a lifetime of savings, and you think, I've had a good life and I'm going to start giving more. I don't have any more demands for my money. My house is paid off; my car is paid off; I can give more money then.

## Reflection: Let No One Off the Hook

Stewardship takes the form of fearless leadership at St. Paul. In Pastor Robert Page, this UCC congregation has a leader who, like ACC's Richard Olmsted, believes that "part of our major problem as a denomination is that we do not call our people to commitment." The Gospel, he reminded me, does not ask for "ten minutes on Sunday but asks for your entire life." While some critics of mainline denominations attribute membership decline to a "too-liberal theology," Page doesn't see it that way. As is the case at Acton Congregational, evangelical churches are by no means models for this pastor:

> I think you can be an ultraliberal and give your whole life. I'm not sure a conservative theology has anything to do with commitment. That has to do with how I read the Gospel. One of the magazines I read regularly, one I really enjoy, is *Sojourners*, which is a solid, evangelical, almost fundamentalist, ultraliberal magazine, because the commitment they talk about is to social justice. Now there are many gifts of the Spirit, and there are many ways that we interpret and hear God's message. I'm not going to say the Assemblies [of God] are wrong. They don't speak to me, but they're not wrong; they have gifts, and I need to hear them because they challenge me. And they need to hear me because I challenge them. But God isn't calling me to any less commitment than he calls them. I think that as long as the UCC waters down that call, we're going to have watered-down commitment.

Page is not averse to the traditional theological bedrocks of justification and sanctification. God may justify him and he may be among the elect, but "it is only as I live out sanctification and grow in that, that I receive the benefits of election, which are peace, joy, freedom." With these, he says, one will likely live a little longer, and "your families are probably going to be a lot more stable." But the key is "the commitment to live the Word." Within St. Paul Church, he says, "faith is the diversity of hearing God's message," which is rich and full, asking, "How do we live in harmony with one another? And hence, different people in this church hear the word very differently. And yet we share together. But none of this lessens the commitment for each one of us."

I drove away from the church reflecting that, yes, Rob Page had been there only three and a half years. But he was beginning to communicate his vision—tolerance of diversity with commitment—and had obviously gained the respect of his parishioners. This vision underlay his version of stewardship, which involves, in part, challenging his congregation to greater generosity with both their money and their time. He is unafraid to rub some members the wrong way now and again. His success shines forth in gradually increasing church revenues and in the surprising success of "Miracle Sundays." Concern for members' spiritual growth leads him to let no one off the hook. Generosity with one's gifts, material and spiritual, is a measure of how seriously one takes the Gospel and lives it out, both through personal growth in Christ and through commitment to one's community. In addition, this pastor evinces a great appreciation of his congregation's generosity as volunteers for ministries to the needy in the community. He is also quick to acknowledge as expressions of stewardship the members' everyday contributions to the city, county, and state in which they live and work, and to the larger UCC. It is little wonder that Robert Page voiced satisfaction in being "pastor of one of the flagship congregations in the denomination."

## CHAPTER 3

# Programs for Children and Youth Attract New Families

*Woodmont Christian Church, Nashville, Tennessee*

With the tallest steeple and spire in Nashville, Woodmont Christian Church stands out to residents and visitors alike. Woodmont, a congregation of the Disciples of Christ, has long been a church representing established Nashville leaders in business, health care, finance, songwriting, and political life. But when the Rev. Douglas Lofton was called to be senior minister in late 1992, he walked into a church of 1,000 members about to celebrate its 50th year of existence but still feeling the effects of recent strife.

> Five years ago the church went through an implosion, I would say, in terms of its identity. It manifested itself in a staff war. The financial end of the church began to dry up, based upon dissatisfaction with the lack of direction for the ministry . . . the year prior to my coming, the outreach for this congregation was less than $10,000.

The turmoil was related to a major change in the congregation. Several old-line families "had basically controlled the church." Even though the church had grown significantly in recent decades, "it refused to function as a program or superprogram church or corporate church. It was still pastor-centered or patriarchal." The consequences were clear to Lofton:

> All this meant that there was a lot of ownership among just a few people, which meant financially they also had a significant commitment to the church. But these families have kind of moved away. Second or third generations of those families are still here, but they don't have the same need for—I don't know if I want to use the word "control"—but they don't have the same need and

desire to be the pivotal people around [whom] the church has ministry or upon whom the church is dependent. Those needs don't exist. So as that has happened, I would say we are probably closer to 70-30, with 70 percent of the budget being raised off of 30 percent of the giving. So we are moving toward a flatter process, which I think is a much healthier process.

Although the turmoil had begun to subside by early 1992 with formulation of a new mission statement and a new constitution and bylaws, Lofton took advantage of the great Mississippi River flood of 1992 to initiate greater member involvement and broaden the scope of participation beyond "the old guard."

Things had begun to improve the first year I was here [1993]. Our giving went from $10,000 to $90,000. But more than that, we set up a separate committee called Church in Community, whose idea was to put hands and feet into work opportunities for this congregation's involvement in their community. As fate would have it, or as God would lead us, our first opportunity was to go to Hull, Illinois, to help build homes for some of the flood victims. I was aware of Hull because it was about 40 miles from where I grew up in Keokuk, Iowa. We went with about 30 of our church members and helped rebuild three homes. These were mostly younger members who came back absolutely excited about the opportunity to put their faith to work. They were also young leaders. In fact, one of them was the chairman of the congregation. He began to carry a real standard for becoming involved more effectively, not only in what we would call remote ministries—overseas or just ministries we would have to drive to—but also those in our community.

Homebuilding in Hull was honored in a weekend edition of *USA Today* as one of ten projects around the country in its "Making a Difference Today" series.

This article was a real motivator to the congregation, basically a pat on the back to say, you need to continue this. They also gave us a $1,000 check to say, go back to Hull next year and do it all over again. So we did. We completed the project and helped the city become renovated and recover from the flood. And we went back and did five homes with a larger group the following year. That got us into Habitat for Humanity here in Tennessee. We've just completed our sixth home in two years, three on our own, and two in cooperation with ecumenical groups, as well as one with African-American churches.

Ministry outreach, then, has transformed Woodmont in two ways: (1) in attracting and galvanizing younger members into active participation, and (2) in enhancing ministry outreach in the local community.

The outreach component drives who we are in terms of our own inside fund-raising as we challenge the congregation to go from no stewardship or outreach in its funding to the community to, by the year 2000, to be at 20 percent of the total budget. That will be a figure close to $250,000 by that date. And yes, it's a significant dollar figure, but more than that, it's a symbol that we hold up, saying we are more than just a presence on a corner; we have a responsibility to the community around us.

Family ministries are one salient expression of this outreach.

What attracts new families is a ready-made program for children and for youth. We have a preschool that pre-existed my coming here that is a program for 200 children midweek. And then we have a youth program for children first grade through 12th Sunday nights that complements the Sunday-morning educational experience. It has grown from 12 children the first year I was here to approximately 140 children at this point. There's a wide base of adult involvement as well, a wide sense of ownership in terms of children's ministries. Sports leagues, of course–basketball, volleyball, softball teams–are part of what you develop as you continue to offer opportunities to young families and young adults.

Stewardship committee members Robert Ramsey and Sandra Carpenter were equally positive about family outreach. Ramsey said.

There was a period when my age of people were leaving because they felt a definite lack—youth didn't have a place in this church. Right, wrong, or different, that was a strong feeling. A number of my friends left. But now it's one of the real strengths of this church. It's amazing to me to sit back and see how many children are so active in the church.

Carpenter observed,

We have a vacation Bible school, an active Sunday school program that involves probably 200 to 300 children, lots of youth choirs. Now there's a full-time youth director, a full-time director of Christian education—all those things and many more. I can't think of all of them.

As Carpenter saw it, revitalizing Woodmont involved expanding ministry opportunities, especially for newer members.

You have to intentionally change some things. From the way they were, you have to bring new programs involving new people, yes. But you also have to let new people be involved in old programs. This means ways of appointing or electing roles of leadership that are open and intentionally include a certain number—not a quota or anything-but looking for young leadership. And that's what Doug and other leaders in this church have let happen or have facilitated.

Business manager Bob Ligon added,

One way we did was to create a nominating committee from a broad base of members. They come up with a slate of officers who get voted on as a group. And that group has grown because of our reorganization here. So we eliminated the popularity contest of the same group of core members, which had made that core feed on itself and burn people out. Fifteen years ago I never got elected to a board. There were only so many openings. That's all changed now. You can be here as little as six months to a year and be elected to the board.

Robert Ramsey added,

> Yes, all of this has happened because there are so many more
> ministry opportunities to plug into now. The same folks don't feel
> they have to do it all. All this has done a lot to increase steward-
> ship giving because a great number of people, those that had burned
> out, didn't quit giving just because they didn't have all the jobs.
> Their giving level has stayed pretty much the same. But younger
> ones who have taken more interest and assumed more responsi-
> bility have increased their giving because they see more of the
> needs we are supporting.

Committee members were quick to cite, in addition to Habitat for Humanity,
support for the Storefront Ministry Food Bank and the Nashville Union
Rescue Mission. Bob Ligon went further with figures:

> Thirty-five agencies around town are supported by our outreach
> dollars. That's in addition to what goes to the national base of mis-
> sions. Plus the outreach budget as a percentage of our total budget
> is increasing every year. And that was intentionally done. A great
> selling point now is to say, "Hey, look what we've done. We've
> ratcheted up our outreach budget each year. That means we're
> doing more in your community. It's all right here; it stays here." It's
> a joy to watch the 20 people on that outreach committee go out and
> do research, and when those solicitations for new ministries come
> in, they look at the projects and say, are they worthwhile? I mean,
> this is not the old, "Well, we gave them some last year, let's do it
> again."

## Pledging and Giving

Pledging had been a tradition in this church. It continues. As in many
churches, once pledge cards are returned, a telephone committee contacts
those who have not yet returned their cards. Very few refuse to pledge.
One member on the phone committee observed,

> Some of our older members, those on fixed incomes, are concerned
> about pledging because they're not quite sure they can fully fund

their pledge, and they don't want to come up short. They would rather just give every Sunday. Some younger couples are in the same boat, hesitant to pledge because they're not sure they can meet it.

When I asked Pastor Lofton what proportion of households made a pledge, he remarked that in the Disciples tradition, large churches usually practice pledging.

> Within the participating membership of this church, I would be willing to say 60 to 70 percent of our participating membership makes a pledge to the congregation. Participating membership is defined here as being involved in at least two different Sundays a month and contributing financially to the church. So someone that just shows up once a year or just gives five dollars once a year isn't a participating member. Of course, this definition raises the percentage of people who are pledging.

*Woodmont supports a variety of ministries. Do they motivate people to pledge and increase giving?*

> Oh, I think it's the key, the critical element. If they understand their dollars are making a difference in the community and in the world, I think that's a significant motivation for people to give. People want, especially affluent people, to give. You know, it's interesting—even though we Disciples are not theologically a guilt-generating denomination, people carry a lot of guilt about wealth. And if they know they are able to make a difference in people's lives who are not as well off as they are, it is a strong motivation to give to organizations who are doing that responsibly.

Pastor Lofton insisted that he did not know and "made it a point not to know" who pledged what amounts.

> I suggest that each person look at where they are and consider what God would have him or her do. Or how would they naturally respond to this gift that's already been given to them. "What is your response to the magnificent gift of God's grace in your life?" And I

don't say, "Is it $5 a week or $10 a week?" I just raise the question and let them begin to deal with it in terms of their own lives.

*How often do you give stewardship sermons?*

I don't preach what I would call specific stewardship sermons more than two times a year. We raise our money in the spring, since we're a fiscal-year-operated church. So in February and March they'll hear those specific sermons. But it isn't an unusual message that they're hearing. They've heard the message in other ways. I don't necessarily define some of my messages as stewardship sermons, but I would hope that at least one out of every three or four sermons calls into question what it means to be good stewards.

*Do you consider stewardship countercultural to the consumer culture?*

Absolutely. From that perspective it certainly is. It's a radical idea for lots of people. It's a response with no strings attached. When we give to the ministry of the church, we do not give because, again, of what we think we will get out of the process. It is a gift of gratitude. That is definitely, I think, countercultural.

## Small-Group Ministries

Pastor Lofton was especially pleased with the growth of small-group ministries at Woodmont. He claimed that "studies showed" that if people's only connection to the worship community was the Sunday worship service itself, "the likelihood of them being there longer than six to 12 months is minimal." People need points of connection or "their faith journey is superficial at best." The church was about to hire an assistant pastor specializing in small-group ministry:

Bible study and spiritual nurturing are so important. These types of adult programs meet with the greatest response. We have probably six or seven small-group men's Bible studies groups meeting anywhere from downtown Nashville to homes to our church proper.

The women's groups, "Connection," flourish, too. These are along-side the more traditional small groups, women's fellowship, and similar men's groups. The newer groups center around personal development and understanding of personal ministries: what we are called to as individuals, our responsibilities, what has God gifted us with? One of the things Disciples have as an advantage is that we claim to be a priesthood of all believers–which means that all persons are thought to be ministers on a daily basis in our homes and in our work. If people embrace that and understand it, it has significant impact on how they lead their lives.

*What proportion of your congregation is involved in these groups?*

At this point, probably no more than 20 percent are tied in. But this is a relatively new occurrence. It's happening at a grassroots level now with very little leadership being offered in the process. The new minister will certainly help a great deal. These groups are getting large enough now that it does require, just from the utilization of space and calendaring issues, a staff person to over-see and coordinate the process, and invite new people into it; also [to] help establish new groups to meet individual needs.

By late 1998, Woodmont had grown to 1,300 members, with an aver-age of 450 attending worship services during fall and spring, and was expanding accordingly. An education and community ministry building was being planned for 2000. The blueprint called for including a 200-seat chapel, allowing for more than one worship service to run concurrently on Sunday morning.

Pastor Lofton refers to Woodmont's commitment to establishing a "south campus" of the church in Franklin, Tennessee, to be staffed initially from Woodmont and later to become a separate Disciples congregation.

Lofton's earlier hopes were fulfilled: A steady yearly increase in total operating receipts from 1996 through the following two years resulted in a 1998 figure of $1,000,979, well over $1,000 per household. By 1998 Woodmont's outreach commitment had reached its goal of 20 percent of total receipts, or a minimum of $250,000 for ministries in 1999. Ministry expansion, for example, included introduction of the Kerygma program, a yearlong intensive course of Bible study. As Lofton wrote to me, "We hoped for 50 participants in five groups. We were pleased that 125 people committed. We currently have nine groups meeting."

## Reflection: Ministry Beyond Church Walls

"Stewardship" under Doug Lofton's pastorate reflects his small-town Iowa upbringing. He recalls a mix of "fairly strong Midwestern values stressing that you were your own person and had to make your own way," together with a faith-filled family that valued activity within the local Disciples church. Stewardship grew naturally in this setting:

> The whole middle-American issue of self-determination was blended with an understanding of God's presence and a responsibility to be thankful back to God for what you had. Being raised in a family of community leaders and church leaders, the blending of the two was a natural process. So understanding the responsibility of the church in terms of an act of force within the community, in terms of making a difference for the marginalized was something I learned early in life.

Seminary experience only amplified what he learned from home and church in small-town Iowa. Lexington Theological Seminary, in Lexington, Kentucky, offered several major tracks of study.

> One of the tracks was social ethics. This track was probably the only one that really tried to identify the idea of a healthy church as one that is constantly seeking to minister beyond its own walls. That was the track that was most attractive to me because it matched up with my own understanding of how God works and what the church's responsibility is to the community.

Salient in this church, it seems to me, is stewardship as growth in evangelistic outreach accompanied by careful financial planning to ensure a resource base for this effort. Lofton's call to Woodmont meant encountering a church that had the resource potential to fulfill the ideal of a "church seeking to minister beyond its own walls." As he put it,

There was a financial tradition here stemming from this church being a wealthy congregation—predominantly professionals, management positions, lawyers, political leaders, company owners. So they've always had a lot of dollars.

As the preceding account makes clear, Lofton used the occasion of the Mississippi flood to turn the younger leadership generation in the direction of his ideal of ministry outreach not just "afar," but to the local community in Nashville. The remarks of stewardship committee members suggest that, in effect, he took a leaf from Peter Block's concept of empowering those whom he served as pastor by refusing to make decisions for them. How he managed instead is strikingly expressed by Charles Henklin, a committee member:

Totally decentralized. Doug's philosophy is to pick good people, whether staff people or those assisting in the selection of division chairs plus the elected leadership, and empower them with responsibility and authority to do their job. And [he] gets out of the way. He's there to support them if they need it, but he doesn't interject his personal attitudes, other than just the confidence he has in those divisions. I'd say he's a good judge of character. He picks good people.

This path of empowerment blends with expanding local ministry outreach and growth in small-group formation to engender member enthusiasm for service. Moreover, financial generosity is enhanced in a congregation already imbued with a volunteer ethos. Once more from Henklin:

Given the professional makeup of this congregation, they're used to doing volunteer service within the community. They find the avenues to serve. I think now when they make contributions, they see their money at work. Not only programs *within* the congregation, but there's a real sense of pride in the *outreach* of this church. It's very substantial from a percentage standpoint and not just a dollar standpoint. And taking on new projects—the way they jump into it is incredible. They see something that needs to be done and they go for it, full steam ahead. Many have been raised in a situation to share and give back to the community. And this is an avenue for that to take place.

Old patterns of giving have been transformed by renewed stewardship planning. Lofton noted that money had always been forthcoming for certain goals, but giving stopped there.

> They could raise a million in a year for a new building, but couldn't probably raise $10,000 for an outreach project or $30,000 for a new staff position. The outreach has been driven in my four years here by the stewardship part of who we are. The budget I received when I first came was in line with where the church had been approximately two years before the crisis here. It was about a half-million-dollar budget. This year our operational income is close to $950,000. We have exceeded our expected budget amount in each of the last four years—which is why we've been able to go back and offer outreach opportunities to our community. It's been exciting to see that happen.

Lofton is understandably proud that Woodmont in 1996 was the seventh-largest-giving Disciples church in the United States. "We have a goal that by the year 2005 we will be the largest giver to Basic Mission Finance in the denomination—that's our unified promotion, our giving to the general offices." Woodmont was also one of the top five churches in giving to "Reconciliation," a special offering to ministries focusing on inner-city racial issues around the nation. Lofton is aware that potential controversy underlies supporting the denominational missions in general versus supporting a specific mission field. The denomination, he noted, is once more considering making available specific ministries for congregations to support:

> And I think that's very attractive to congregations—not limiting at all. But I also think we lean here toward not giving as much dollar support to specific ministries as we do to the broader church. So that's a balancing act. We'll have to see how it plays itself out.

Endowments sometimes generate controversy among pastors and denominational officials, with the suggestion that they depress regular giving and pledging. Woodmont has a half-million-dollar endowment. "We are currently in [the] process of accepting a goal of a $10 million endowment by the year 2000." Part will be used for local-ministry outreach, another, perhaps, for capital expenses, "and possibly a small portion could be designated as seed money for new ministries," underwriting a ministry for one or two years, after which operational dollars would support it. Lofton seems determined to avoid turning endowment proceeds into operational funds. At the end of each fiscal year,

> we try to be fiscally sound, yes, but also try to make sure that the money that's come in has obviously gone out. No large reserves. We don't believe in them. An endowment should expand ministry, not ensure it.

A final personal note: I accepted Doug Lofton's invitation to attend the more informal 9 A.M. Sunday worship service geared to the congregation's younger members, including families with their children. Lofton dressed in jeans rather than donning a robe, sat on a stool and spoke and preached informally to us. Though I was reminded of megachurch services I have attended, this service was anything but casually organized and conducted, and steered away from self-conscious "folksiness." Informal though it was, the service indeed conveyed a reverent sense of expectancy. Congregational members obviously enjoyed the participation of the children in readings and song. A church gracefully adapting to its changing environment, I thought.

Big mainline churches are in trouble? Not growing or expanding? Obviously that's not the case with this one.

## CHAPTER 4

# GOD HAS CALLED US
# TO BE PARTNERS IN MINISTRY

*Christian Church of Arlington Heights, Illinois*

"In the three congregations I have served, this idea of invitation and encouraging people to commit their resources, time, talent, and money have been an integral part of my approach to ministry," says the Rev. Daniel Webster. He is pastor of a church of 263 members or approximately 85 households (as of 1996) in one of greater Chicago's northwestern suburbs (population 81,000). It is a congregation of the Christian Church (Disciples of Christ). Arlington Heights, says Webster, is "a mostly white-collar suburb. We have some management-type people, but lots of teachers, electronic technicians. Not very many professionals, though. I'd have to say we're white ethnically, too; three African-Americans and two Koreans are members." Ten years ago he succeeded a pastor who had strongly supported stewardship, "so people were used to hearing about money and time and talents." Dan met denominational stewardship consultants and learned from them by attending "a couple of conferences in which there was further training in the area."

Nine years ago, he asked church members to consider a tithe through a "Grow One" program, which suggests that parishioners give thought to their present giving, then work gradually toward a full tithe at the pace of a one percent increase per year. Dan's convictions arose from previous pastoral experience—what was helpful in the stewardship of money and what was not:

> I don't want us to say, "Here's your fair share." I don't want us to say, "Here's the budget; we've got to meet it." Also I didn't want us, particularly in that first go-around, to fail; no sense that what we were doing had collapsed. So the first year [that] we looked at the "Grow One" campaign, we said, we'll set our budget afterwards. You can't fail if you haven't got a target, and of course, we

just blew the top out of what we received the year before. Asking people to respond to what God had done in their lives, then respond to what God has done in your life *and* consider increasing giving by one percent—those two things converged in that first campaign.

"Grow One" is neither a demand nor an expectation, he says. "But it is an issue that we've continued to raise ever since: 'Stop, Look, Can You Grow One?'" Webster and his wife did decide to go the full 10 percent themselves, but he admits that as a childless couple, they enjoy degrees of freedom not shared by parents of children still at home. Full tithing, then, is more likely to be found "among people who are pretty mature." He knows that allowances must be made:

> I acknowledge the fact there are folks in different positions able to give different things. For example, we have what somebody referred to as "spiritually single people." I'm not sure I like that term, but they are members of a family where the spouse does not attend church. So the purse strings are held pretty tightly by, say, a husband who doesn't attend church at all. The money is not hers alone (or his, in some cases) to give large amounts, because of the spouse. In this situation, I feel I have to acknowledge that this person may give an extraordinary amount of *time* in teaching or coming over to church and doing repairs—things that don't cost money that he or she is not able to give freely. I have to recognize the circumstance.

*Is there a danger that some people prefer to give money so they don't have to give time and talent?*

> Oh, sure, that's an issue. This was a church that for many, many years did all its own grass-cutting, did all its own custodial work, all by volunteers. As time went on, the work got concentrated more and more in the hands of a few, and the word came . . . "I would rather give you more money than I would give you time doing those sorts of things."

*If we talk about urging people to give at this level, how important is what the church is doing in terms of ministry in the community?*

Real important. That's why we try to keep people posted on all the things we're involved in—local issues, not heavily, but a few that are significant and we want folks to know what those are. Also, we're very involved in our denomination's work. We do keep an eye out for chances of involvement. Connections are important to us. For instance, if one of our members is working with campus ministries, we look to that person for guidance and suggestions for involvement.

## Ministries

Before coming to Arlington Heights, Dan Webster had worked in disaster relief for Church World Service. "I could talk to parishioners about tornado or flood sites, and people were able to make a connection." It didn't stop there.

Our contributions, what we call here "Week of Compassion" (some of the other mainline denominations will call it "One Great Hour of Sharing"), have traditionally been the highest in the Illinois region of our denomination. For a small congregation, that's pretty good. But we had connections. We sent folks to Jamaica on work trips, and they came back and talked about it. Almost every year, we've tried to bring in a missionary or denominational executive who can talk about where our money is going when we give to the BMF [Basic Mission Finance].

*So giving to the denomination is not an abstraction.*

Not for us. Not at all. And that did not start with me. Goes back at least through the previous pastor and maybe even before him.

*How have you expanded ministries and people's involvement in them since you've been here?*

One of the ways we've done so is simply to encourage people to look at their spiritual and other gifts and find a place where they fit. I remind people that for everyone, that doesn't have to be in the church. We send you forth with our blessings if you have gifts that will help you out at the hospital or tutoring a refugee. [That's] not a church ministry, but your ministry is blessed by the church.

Dan Webster easily named the ministry expressions of his small church: Sunday school teachers, choir members. "People to do this, that and the other: CROP walks, food pantries, Christmas program, gift exchange for poor kids in public housing near the church. We also share our church space with a Korean congregation. But again, ministries don't all happen in the church, and we don't expect them to."

Formal membership is often preceded by involvement in the church. In fact, visitors are invited to get involved. "Arm-twisting or sales techniques" are not a part of this:

And then we make that official. So we'll have somebody who's been a member of a choir, say for a year, join the church. Or from some other ministry join the church. So in our case, we kind of do things backwards. Come join with us, see how you feel about working with us in the ministry. When I go visit people in their homes, I say, "You'll know when it's right. I want you to get as involved in a Sunday school class, a small group as you can. I want you to be involved in any of the work that appeals to you. You'll know when the day is right to come forward and join the church."

The same low-key approach is in play at "Get Acquainted Desserts" held a couple of times a year. People interested in the church become acquainted with the church's ministries in a relaxed and conversational atmosphere.

Ministries, of course, require time spent by volunteers, and it is precisely time crunches that everyone seems to experience these days. All pastors with whom I spoke for this study were aware of how precious day and evening hours were to their members. Some ministry commitments obviously continue much longer than a few hours a week, and these can be truly problematic.

Most of our teachers teach semesters rather than commit for all year long. We give breaks in the summer to our choir and its director. When we do Bible studies, we'll often schedule them in shorter-term chunks like six weeks or eight weeks. You know, take a break and do something else later. But a lot of jobs *are* one-year jobs. And if you come on board as a deacon or elder, it's a three-year job.

Church Board members I interviewed affirmed that this is a "giving church." In contrast to the churches to which some had previously belonged, mission outreach wasn't just something that came up when an occasional missionary would visit the pulpit. A board member remarked,

> When we arrived here, mission outreach was already set in place with the pastor. Reaching out to the whole world was a part of us, and talking to other members here, we became much more aware of the need for us to be aware of that giving. What we understood was, a healthy church is a giving church.

Another observed that when members who have been "good stewards" move, board members tend to believe the loss will depress giving. Instead, "it goes up higher all the time. It's just sort of amazing." The mission in Jamaica also came in for comment:

> We've had people in our church, now including Dan [Webster], who have gone down to Jamaica and helped build schools and parsonages on a work trip. We've supported that for some time now, just as we supported our members who went to help sandbag the Mississippi down in Missouri where the floods were. We all want to help them. All these things I guess can be termed leadership, and it's what makes people want to go on these missions.

Getting junior-high and high-school students involved is always a challenge in any church. The flood-relief mission offered just such a path of involvement. Mentioned with great approval was a skit about the disaster put on by young members, which led one older member to reflect,

> I think you can almost start to see our enthusiasm, and maybe that's what keeps it going. When we start talking about outreach, we simply like to do it. If we were told not to do it, we might just go someplace else where we could!

Local ministry, they reported, is sometimes generated during a single church service. During an interlude called "Concerns" at the Sunday worship service, people make known needs members may want to address. A board member offered an example:

> Denise is a Purdue graduate, and one of her friends was teaching in inner-city Chicago. She had no supplies, nothing, and she needed books. She stood up in church during "Concerns" and just told people all this. So many came up to her. Now she's got a box in fellowship hall. There was just this immediate, "Well, I've got some books here, and I've got some crayons that have been sitting around." In fact, one of the first responses was from a visitor who had never been here before. He came back the next Sunday and brought a whole bunch of stuff with him.

## Attracting Young Adults and Young Families

About eight years ago, Dan Webster asked a question of the very few young adults in the congregation. "I just said, 'OK, there's just you three; where do we go from here?' And we began to be intentional about inviting people." Among the first strategies was setting up a Sunday School class just for young adults. "Many things developed out of that Sunday School class." Not least was the appearance of young musicians who found their way to the church.

> God knows I can't sing and I can't play anything. But the annual music program they've done has been wonderful. Working together, singing together has given them a real solid nucleus. Since we began to attract them, we've had some marriages and had kids. That brings a whole new dynamic of mothers and fathers sharing back and forth with baby-sitting and watching out for one another. Other dynamics seem to have kicked in that none of us would have anticipated, but have made the group grow stronger and faster. In fact, from that group two young adults are now in seminary, entering ministry full-time. We're really excited about that.

Before long, two of the "20-somethings" became elders in the church, having shown "the maturity and leadership ability to be shepherds, leaders in this congregation." Sixty years of age, Webster remarked, is a requisite in some churches to become an elder. Not here:

> We have said, if you show the capability, we will recognize it and honor you by making you what, in essence, you already are. So some of our young adults have been very involved in the upper echelons, if that's a fair word to use, in our church.

A youthful elder affirmed Webster's observations:

> Dan was very instrumental. He preached a sermon one Sunday and said, "This is a good church, but I know we can be better. What are your ideas to make it better?" And I just came up to him and said, "A young-adult group and a young-adult Sunday school class." Now we're distinctive because we have that. In fact, now it's more than that; it's for anyone that feels comfortable there. Then we try to have an activity once a month for young adults. Plus, we've led young-adult worship services. And the congregation has just been—well, they've loved it. They've asked for more. By this time we have taken on deaconing, eldering, all the music. We have such talented people in this church, I mean, just about anybody who could step in and play the piano and the organ—we've taken over everything but the sermon!

The elder was clear that the young-adult program had generated its own momentum:

> It's such a welcoming congregation. Young adults have just grown. And we're trying to do more—that includes the Christmas program. [The] first year we did it, just young adults. The next year it was anyone who wanted to participate, and that's how we've done it. When young adults come here, they see we have seven babies in one year! They just see that there are young families here and that, you know, everybody's mixing. It's not [that] the young families go over here and older people go over there.

From an older member listening in:

> It's apparent you're welcome at any of the young-adult activities. It's not like you feel any more included or excluded if you're not deeply involved in what's going on. It gives families the opportunity to come in for, OK, the Super Bowl party or, OK, we'll be active with the CROP Walk or whatever the program is for that month. I think families feel they can come in and out without necessarily, "Well, I don't belong anymore." It's not like you have to participate all the time, because everybody here has very active schedules. I don't think it matters who you are: high school youth, young adults, or older members. After all, a lot of people drive a good distance to get here. If you're talking about a 20-minute drive, that's a commitment right there!

The youthful elder adds:

> It's a family, and you want to give to see the family continue to grow. This congregation is like my family.

## Pledging and Giving

Pledging has been a long-standing tradition at Christian Church of Arlington Heights. Webster acknowledges occasional resistance from new members. His succinct defense of pledging could serve as a model for any church:

> We simply explain that when you pledge, two things happen: First, the church can look down the road for a full year and say, we have some goals we hope to accomplish; this helps us know whether they're possible. If we can, we're going to chase those goals. If we can't, we'll reduce our expectations accordingly. Second, pledging helps people project and plan what they're going to give. If I anticipate a raise halfway through the year, then maybe for the first half I give "X" amount and after that I'll give "Y" amount. People can plan their giving a lot better.

Most years close to 80 percent of members make a pledge, a remarkably high number. Webster said he could not explain why the percentage of members pledging toward the 1997 budget went down, yet the overall amount pledged rose between 3 percent and 5 percent. Monies received during calendar year 1996 totaled $181,587. While average Sunday worship attendance hovered around 125, church membership in 1996 totaled 263, translating into a per-member yearly giving of $690. A more telling figure arises when we focus on the 172 "participating members," defined in the Year Book Report Form as "only those members who attended, contributed to, or otherwise showed continuing interest in the church during the year." Per-member contribution by this definition comes to $1,056, impressive for any small mainline Protestant congregation.

At the end of January, each donor gets a receipt for the previous year's giving. Pledgers get another report in late June. "Using those two, they know where they stand," says Webster. "No notes saying you're behind. We simply say, here's what you've given to date, and we thank you." Only the financial secretary knows who pledges what. "I really don't want to know," the pastor says.

Webster agreed that stewardship of money is countercultural:

> Many of the people of this church are middle- and upper-middle-class. Most of them, most of us–I should include myself–have financial planners we work with that help us accumulate wealth, as the planner says. Fortunately some of us have found planners who also want to help us distribute that wealth. It's nice when you can find someone who understands that process. But yes, it does run against culture which says, accumulate either wealth or stuff. It doesn't understand this concept of giving it away.

The notion of partnership with God is central to how stewardship is actually preached and taught:

> We talk a lot about partnership, how God has called us to be partners in ministry and the idea of working toward and helping create the Kingdom. And that there is blessing in the partnership and in the relationship we have with God as we do that giving, whether it be of time, talent, or money. And sometimes that's the only reward, the experience of "I have done something right; I

have done something well; I have given to something greater than myself." And I don't think that's an insignificant blessing.

*A kind of intrinsic satisfaction?*

Yes. Of knowing that I am partners with the greatest one of all. John says to know Jesus is eternal life. It's a sense in which I experience eternal life when I am connected with my divine partner, Jesus Christ—when I know that hand in hand, we are doing this thing. To me, giving and reflecting on that is a spiritual experience. And those are few and far enough between so that those are pretty major blessings and rewards.

Committee members echoed Webster's reflections:

As one of us said earlier, a healthy outreach church is a healthy church. They'll do all right with their finances. When they get too selfish, they won't. We think of all this kind of collectively. We have so many blessings that Dan preaches quite a bit on them. It's certainly not a carrot-or-stick kind of preaching.

Members gently pushed aside my probing as to how this small church could support outreach so generously:

In our congregation, stewardship is more a natural process. I don't think we really examine how we come up with the money to help this group over here or that church over there. It's just, OK, they need the help; how can we do it? I think we're afraid that if we try to analyze it, we're going to look too deep and the whole system is going to fall apart! You know, it's a great system; don't try to improve it. We don't fully understand how it works ourselves, how we help somebody else or another church with their problems and with their stewardship.

Small capital campaigns are run through an unusual loan program that surely reflects the "family atmosphere" of this small church.

We asked folks if they would consider loaning us a thousand dollars for up to three years and promised that we would pay back one person a month during those three years, literally by lottery, drawing names out of a hat and developing an order by which folks could be paid back. We pay them back their thousand dollars. Their loan (interest-free) saves the church the interest we would have had to spend going to a savings-and-loan.

One of the unique things about it was, a number of people, when the time came to give them back their money, said "Keep it. I've found that I don't need it." So we got contributions in addition to loans! Because people were generous, we were always able to pay back the money at a much more rapid rate. At one point, we were paying back $3,000 every two months and paid three years off in two. Now I don't think this is the kind of thing I would even bring up if we had several hundred members. But having less than a hundred, we all know each other. I think that trust is there.

Webster praised worship leaders, including musicians, in his congregation, all of whom are unpaid volunteers. They help make possible the church's reputation for high outreach giving. The pastor is proud that, as of 1996, his small church was one of the top 200 Disciples congregations in the United States in giving, both in total dollars and in percent of church income to the denomination's Basic Mission Finance. In 1996, 27 percent of the church's receipts went, in the words of the Year Book Report Form, "to Church Finance Council and to other world, national, or local ministries whether Disciples-related or not." As Webster told his congregation, "Every congregation ahead of us had at least 100 more active members in their congregation than we do." Most strikingly, his church was ranked sixth among Disciples churches nationally in per-capita giving to mission outreach. "We were one of 37 congregations to be recognized in all three of the categories [world, national, and local]. I think that says a lot about who we are as a church and what we understand ourselves to be." Webster is quick to acknowledge the role of church volunteers in these indicators of success:

I point out to the congregation that if we had to pay them, I don't know where the money would come from. The outreach area would have to be cut. And we don't want to do that; we are very grateful to our musicians, but we recognize what they allow us to do otherwise because of their gifts.

## Reflection: Members Who Take Ownership

Well-worn though the word may be, "ownership" best describes the gift
pastor Dan Webster has bestowed on this small church. Christian Church
of Arlington Heights truly exemplifies community-building through invitation. Like his colleague and friend Doug Lofton at Nashville's Woodmont
Church, Webster took seriously a key element stressed by management
consultant Peter Block, cited in the introduction: Stewardship involves
forsaking "parenting" in favor of true community partnership, creating a
compelling sense of value in being a contributing member. I was struck by
the sensitivity Webster displayed over implementing the "Grow One" program, his eminently hands-on methods of ministry development (the trips
to Jamaica and to the Missouri flood victims), and his willingness to ask
young adults how more of their age group could be attracted. Further, he
gave these initiatives a spiritual context: Members were to be partners
with God in making possible the outreach so clearly cherished by congregation members–outreach that expresses stewardship for them.

What stands out is the enthusiastic momentum this approach generates within a congregation, taking the form of pride and joy in realizing
that it has become a family whose members easily cross the generational
boundaries that some churches find troublesome. That the church is small
enough to generate personal closeness and family spirit–"we all know one
another"–is certainly part of the picture.[1] So is musical excellence. In combination these factors help explain the cadre of unpaid volunteers that
many a church would envy. But pastoral leadership, grounded in the servant model advocated by stewardship proponents, has been a key factor
here. Interviews with church members and officers make this factor evident. The emerging portrait, consonant with both secular and religious
stewardship literature, is that of a congregation become aware that ministries, innovations in worship service, and new expressions of outreach are
theirs to suggest, implement, and improve. Theirs is the responsibility. All
are gifts to be developed in partnership with God to advance the Kingdom. It is no surprise that Christian Church of Arlington Heights is truly a
dynamic congregation and that it provides a persuasive stewardship model
for any small church to consider.

CHAPTER 5

# WE'RE A SEVEN-DAY-A-WEEK CHURCH

*First Institutional Baptist Church, Phoenix, Arizona*

Where to begin is a daunting question with this wonderful church, First Institutional Baptist of Phoenix. I remember a blur of activity as I drove into the parking lot on a Thursday afternoon. My eye caught young people intermingling with adults, a sure sign of a vital congregation. Then a warm greeting from an assistant pastor: "You're here to talk to Pastor Stewart, right?" Aware of halls and offices full of people, I was led to the office of the Rev. Dr. Warren H. Stewart, Sr., who noticed my attention to walls filled with photographs. I had embarked on one of my most memorable church-visit weekends to this African-American congregation of 2,600 members.

Before turning to Pastor Stewart, let me describe my most striking impression of this church, resonating a full two years after my visit: It is indeed a house of prayer. In fact, FIBC (as members call it) literally has a School of Prayer whose dean, The Rev. Jackie L. Green, is responsible (with a great deal of help) for organizing the following "FIBC Prayer Ministry Opportunities." The school's mission statement emphasizes the primacy of intercessory prayer:

> The FIBC School of Prayer is designed to equip and train members (all age levels) in the Body of Christ how to become active witnesses through individual and corporate intercession, thusly affecting their home, church, community, nation and world for the sake of the Kingdom of God.

FIBC "Prayer Ministry Opportunities" for members include the following:

1. *Upper Room Prayer.* During each of the two Sunday services (7:45 A.M. and 11 A.M.), volunteers pray in a room over the sanctuary for the success of the services being held below them.

2. *JTP ("Just to Pray")*. Every Wednesday from 6:30 to 7:30 P.M., church members are invited to a prayer service in the sanctuary under the motto, "Through prayer we can become the 'Hope of the City.'" As Pastor Stewart notes at the outset of the program distributed at the service, "In a time when our schedules are 'full before we get there,' Jesus calls us to a special place of intercession and prayer." The program includes praying for the world, for all nations, the United States, the city of Phoenix, and the state of Arizona, plus members' own petitions for families and special needs. "Handle Phoenix with Prayer" heads page 6 of the program which, along with listing city officials and leaders, also cites "Strongholds in the City that need to be broken by prayer." Examples are "the spirit of racism and prejudice, the spirit of witchcraft and the occult, . . . the spirit of leisure (laziness), the spirit of violence (gangs, crime), drugs, the spirit of division and competition among churches, and the spirit of perversion (prostitution/homosexuality)." This church's theology embraces the belief that "building the Kingdom of God through Jesus Christ our Lord on earth" must be accompanied by "tearing down strongholds" of the satanic enemy.

3. *The FIBC Prayer Calendar*. Each day of the month is dedicated to a subject of prayer. A few examples: "Bless the Earth and Pray for Environment"; "For the Fruits of the Spirit and Gifts of the Spirit"; "Family Ministry, Singles Ministry, Christian Couples"; "Pastor Stewart"; "Revival and Outpouring on our Men, Promise Keepers, Men's Retreats, Classes, and Conference."

4. *A 24-hour Prayer Line*. It is run with church-member volunteers.

A couple of months before I arrived, Jackie Green organized the "First Annual FIBC Prayer Conference," lasting five days. Attenders were led in intercessory prayer to open each day. Seminars followed; e.g., "How to Pray for Pastors and Leaders," "Fasting and Prayer as a Lifestyle," "Help for Those Wounded in Warfare," "62 Ways to Get Your Church to Pray," "Healing Ministry in our Churches," and "The Lifestyle of an Intercessor."

Prayer, then, is the very center ministry of FIBC. Between the two Sunday services, I attended a class in prayer. About 25 people were present. The young woman teacher led us through the four basic types of prayer: adoration, thanksgiving, petition, and contrition, offering examples of each and encouraging our questions.

Closely related to the School of Prayer is the "Christian Studies Institute," through which classes are offered (including the one I attended). During the fall trimester of 1996, eight classes were offered between the two Sunday services. Three were offered on Tuesday evenings, two on Thursday evenings, two on Saturday mornings and one (called noonday Bible study) each Wednesday during the lunch hour. Topics included men's studies, women's studies, "Before You Say I Do" (for the engaged and about-to-be-married), two courses labeled "Survival Kit I" and "Survival Kit II" (helping members "become involved in a consistent Bible study"), CWT (continuing witnessing training) classes, and "Cult and Occult Evangelism" to explore "some of the current misconceptions and teachings of false witnesses and opponents of the Gospel of Jesus Christ."

Little doubt remained that I was visiting a strongly evangelical church. Pastor Stewart extended a warm welcome. Photographs on the walls spoke to the pastor's community activism. I paused before one of Stewart standing with the mayor of Phoenix. "He was pleased that I led the struggle in Phoenix to get Martin Luther King Day recognized in the only state that didn't [observe it] at the time." This church of prayer was also a church of community outreach.

## A Tithing Church

Working up to a full tithe is an ideal preached and encouraged at FIBC. I wondered how Warren Stewart had come to embrace tithing.

> Stewardship and tithing never came up in seminary, but when I was 17 and converted shortly afterwards, I was a member of a Baptist church but attending a Church of God in Christ, which was Pentecostal. One night I went to a nondenominational revival. The evangelist who was on that night was dealing with giving and tithing. He said, "God wants his people to tithe." I'd never been approached about tithing that way. And I said, this is something I am supposed to do, and it's in God's word. I'm going to do it. So I simply started. For me—and I tell everybody—tithing is one of the easiest things I do as a Christian because it's based on a mathematical formula, so it's no guesswork. Tithing is giving 10 percent of your income.

*You mean the first check you write . . . ?*

Yes, sir, without a doubt. I develop a personal budget each year. At the top is not taxes; the top is tithe.

*How about introducing tithing here at FIBC?*

Let's start with the concept the Lord gave me called Fund for Missions. After being here around three months, I challenged this church because the church really didn't give to missions. In African-American churches [on] the fifth Sunday in times past, that's been Mission Sunday. Well, historically, that's been little old ladies in white dresses taking up penny offerings. So I started Fund for Missions, and I said, "Let's take 5 percent off the top of the church's income." Like if we received $1,000 the first Sunday, take $50 and set it aside in a fund for missions. Let us give at least 5 percent to home missions, foreign missions, education, and special projects. I set up a committee to oversee this. And still now, after 19 years, every fourth Sunday, we put in the bulletin our Fund for Missions report. By now it has increased above 10 percent. So I moved then to urge people to become *individual* tithers at 10 percent. I said, the same biblical principle that says God will bless the tither [means] he will bless a church that tithes. So we moved over the years from 5 percent to 10 percent-plus. In a word, First Institutional tithes off the top of its income at least 10-plus percent to all types of mission causes, causes that we as a church designate.

*What are some of the missions and special projects the church funds through mission giving?*

We send some to [the] American Baptists, some to [the] National Baptists; we have a lot of local projects. We run a home for teenage unwed mothers; we run a Samaritan House, which is an emergency shelter for the homeless; we have a corporation called FIBCO Family Services, which tries to help people get jobs; another program gives thousands of dollars in scholarships. We built a church in Soweto, South Africa, dedicated in 1993. All these come out of our mission budget.

*Is there enough surplus, so to speak, to generate other newer missions from time to time?*

Oh, yes. We have a catchall category called undesignated mission causes. So when something comes up like the hurricane in Florida a few years ago, I asked people to join me—"Who will give $100?" They gave $22,000 extra on one Sunday for that cause. We gave $10,000 the same way for something else that came up two or three years ago.

*Now, what proportion of your households tithe?*

About 20 percent tithe the full 10 percent. But amazingly, the more people make, the less they give to the church. My consistent tithers—well, there are several middle-income families, but I'm really talking about lower-middle-income, lower-income, people on Social Security checks, on retirement checks, and minimum-wage jobs. Now I do have several professionals who give substantial tithes because their incomes are high.

*Some pastors don't want to know the identity of tithers. What about you?*

I do not look at individual giving records because I don't want that to affect how I think of people or my relationship with people, since I do think one evidence of spiritual commitment or maturity is his or her giving. Now I do get a list, probably twice a year, of the tithers, so that way I do know who they are, but I don't know how much they give. The list of tithers is useful because, for example, I would not recommend a trustee for the church who is not a tither. Trustees handle the church's money. My philosophy is, how can you handle the church's money if you're not tithing on your own? So only tithers are recommended to be trustees. They are my financial oversight committee, rotating every three years.

*Do you preach frequently about tithing or is there a certain time of year . . . ?*

Well, November's usually stewardship month, where I talk about giving, thanksgiving, and God-response tithing. So I do preach about it directly, yes. But every Sunday either myself or someone else receives the tithes and offerings. I may say a word or two then about how well we're doing and how we have to keep giving. From time to time one of our staff ministers preaches about tithing. We have what we call "Tithing Testimonies"–lay members who tithe come up and say why they are tithers. But it's quick, about 90 seconds, and they say a prayer and receive tithes and offerings.

*You mentioned earlier that blessings come to a tithing church. But is it your practice to preach tithing in terms of the individual or the family–God's going to return blessings if you tithe?*

That's not my first point. It's always that we tithe out of thanksgiving for what God has already done. Malachi 3:10 says, bring the full tithe to the storehouse. The Lord will open up the windows of heaven and pull you out a blessing that you will have received. Now I don't emphasize the opening up the windows of heaven. I emphasize, look what God has already done because he has blessed you with an income or health or whatever. You should tithe for what he has *already* done.

*So it's a response.*

Yes. Now, I do throw in that he does say, if you do tithe, he will give you all kinds of blessings. I don't mean material blessings. He will bless you in many ways. But I don't push that if you do this, you're going to get that. I push, look what he has already done. Tithing for me is an act of thanksgiving. Now this doesn't mean people want to hear about giving. You asked me why more pastors don't adopt a stewardship approach: because people in the pews don't want to hear it. The most challenging preaching I do is on giving, because the moment you mention "tithe," you can feel the walls go up in the sanctuary. Here, even though we spend about 90 seconds on a Sunday mentioning tithes and offerings, we still get some of this "All they talk about is money." So many people, even though we have a growing number of tithers, don't want to hear this message. On the other hand, as more people decide to tithe, some ask me, "Pastor, when are you going to preach on tithing again?" But you know, a lot of pastors who do stewardship say, "OK, you're not going to get full tithers, so ask people to give 5 percent. Or 3 percent." Naw. I go for the 10 percent.

Parishioners know Stewart tithes. Not long after he arrived, the church treasurer, who had been a member for 17 years, pulled him aside and remarked that he was the first pastor ever who didn't just preach tithing but also practiced it. Stewart noted to me that while tithing, he and his wife are also raising six children and supporting two in college. "And I'm prepared for this."

Of no small importance is that church revenues have enabled the pastor and his congregation to meet the challenge of a building drive through "double-tithing."

We have a property expansion fund. Take our administration building. Back in 1984, we wanted to build it. We began to tithe to the expansion fund just for this building. We literally double-tithed: 10 percent off the top for missions, then we'd take another 10 percent for the expansion fund. And [we] didn't stop meeting our operating expenses.

Deacon Mark Smith knows he has benefited from tithing. As one of the more substantial givers in the church (he owns two very successful barbecue restaurants that draw NFL football teams when they play in Phoenix), his is the attitude of a cheerful giver.

*Would you say God rewards you for tithing?*

I would rather say he blesses me, yes. You are denying yourself something, but first of all, it already belongs to God from the beginning of time when God created the heavens and the earth. So everything that dwells within is God's. He just put us in control of it. And then we go from there.

*But you don't want materially because you tithe?*

I don't look at the material side of it. I look at the blessing side. There is health, strength; my family is healthy and strong. I have a sense of peace knowing that if there's something I go to the Lord in prayer for, he'll come through for me. So I bless God back with what he's already given me. By me paying my tithe, I know that the church will be able to operate and be able to reach out to other people who are in need. By the way, I teach my children to tithe, too. When I take them down to the business to work, I pay them; then they have to pay their 10 percent tithe on that.

Mark Smith commended Pastor Stewart for preaching that those not tithing "are missing out on the blessing" that follows a decision to tithe. He mentioned the New Testament's "widow's mite," elaborating with his own eloquence:

That woman, if she has that much faith, man, that's serious. To me that's serious.

*Taking your belief seriously?*

Yes, yes. It's stepping out in faith. I try to do it as a discipline. Before I write any check, my first check is my tithe check. First fruit, right off the top. Then I just walk in peace and I walk in confidence because I know that God is there for me.

Casual conversations after the 7:45 A.M. Sunday worship service suggested strongly that Mark Smith isn't the only happy tither at FIBC. Sociologists in recent years have discussed the quality of "seriousness" in forms of religious commitment, often predicating this quality of evangelical churches. First Institutional Baptist struck me as a "serious" church in every sense possible.

## Stewardship, Volunteering and Ministries

I asked Pastor Stewart what it took to become a member of this church.

Well, believe in Jesus Christ as Lord and Savior. And to unite and say you want to be a part of FIBC. We have four new-member classes they're required to attend that deal with different aspects of being a Christian. Then, on the first Sunday night of the month, we have communion, the Lord's Supper, and new members receive what we call the right hand of fellowship. That's the last act of membership, and then we vote them in symbolically.

Stewart conceives of stewardship holistically. It embraces an ideal he expresses with simple eloquence:

Stewardship does include giving of one's time and talent, yes; but more than that, it means your total life. One's whole life should be that of being a steward. We are not even owners of our lives. God has loaned us our lives. And so we are responsible to him in how we take care of ourselves, how we are healthwise. Being a good steward is not having bad health habits! Giving financially is just one portion of stewardship.

*Volunteers these days are often hard to come by for churches. Moms and dads are both working, including single parents. How do you motivate people to volunteer for ministries?*

By meeting their needs. People respond if their needs are being met, whether it's parenting, whether it's children and youth, whether it's a senior program, a substance-abuse program, a support-group ministry, whatever. People respond as those needs are met. If there's a need that we're not meeting, we create a new ministry to meet that need. We have some 70 ministries at this congregation, and that's not enough. I mean, if there's a new need that comes up tomorrow and we can find people to meet it, we'll take care of it.

*You seem to have an extensive staff here.*

I have four assistant pastors and around 12 other full-time paid staff. We also have some part-time people. But take my assistant pastors: I have a minister of administration and development who runs the day-to-day administrative tasks. I have a minister of evangelism and discipleship. I have a minister of prayer and pastoral counseling, a director of AACTS, our African-American Christian

Training School. And that's in addition to a minister of children, youth, and young adults. Then I have an assistant in visitation and social service ministries, which is like a half-time position. Then another half-time post, which is minister of music. Three of those ministers are seminary-trained: evangelism; children, youth, and young adults; and pastoral counseling.

Stewart underscored the importance of FIBC's extensive Bible study program, reflecting the belief that once one becomes a convert, yet another step is in order: becoming a disciple or learner–thus the large number of courses taught on Sunday between services and during the week. As mentioned above, the Christian Studies Institute is the church's alternative to the traditional Sunday school, but much more elaborate and structured in its three trimesters of courses. "Several hundred," Stewart affirmed, are enrolled in any given trimester. Classes are taught wholly by volunteers. Enough new members were coming into the church to warrant a projected third worship service, targeting those to whom many churches are paying attention:

> We're thankful that new members are coming, and that's why we're going to start a Saturday night service. It will reach a group we call "seekers," people who are leery of traditional church. So it will be [a] totally contemporary, dress-down, no-suit-and-tie, fast-moving service to reach out to the Generation X crowd, 30-ish and down.

No justice could be done to FIBC without mentioning the ministry of street preaching. Deacon Mark Smith's reply to my question about the "most impressive ministries the church engages in" left no doubt about his priority:

> Street witnessing. I'm a part of that. Out of anything I do in this church, I get the most out of street witnessing. You know, going out knocking on doors, passing out "door hangers" [biblical messages imprinted on cards with hooks to hang on doorknobs], spreading the good news of Jesus Christ. Helping out people. I mean emancipation, evangelization. Trying to let people know that Jesus Christ is for real.

*Well, what do you say to people you meet?*

"My name is Mark Smith and I'm out here today sharing the good news of Jesus Christ. Do you have a moment, a second that I could just share a few words with you?" And then I just start up a conversation, ask a few questions. We have a little "Eternal Life" pamphlet and different things to hand them from our church. Then we try to see if they can get to some church home, not just First Institutional, but just somewhere they can go to start serving the Lord. And try to get them to accept Jesus Christ as their personal Saviour. Oh yes, our team goes out every Saturday like for two hours. And I take my kids with me, too. No reason at all they can't be involved. Then another deacon and I go every second Friday of the month to homeless shelters, and we bring them down in busloads, vanloads. We feed them and we spread the Good News.

## Youth Ministries

Mark Smith has seen youth programs double since the arrival of the Rev. Anthony W. Green, minister of children, youth, and young adults. Smith is convinced that kids "are looking for something." If they don't get "something positive," they will "get off on something negative." The important thing is reaching out:

Those kids are our future. And if we as adults don't reach out to them, then they'll be a lost generation. But they don't have to be. It's left up to us to do the reaching out.

Smith and his wife work with the youth choirs. He also hires young people in his business and would like to hire more.

Right now I have 33 employees. My goal is to have 100. And I get children from all different ethnic backgrounds. I get them to come in and work together. In fact, my customers are from all different ethnic backgrounds, too, as you'll see if you go out there.

Among the goals for youth ministry programs are "designed fellowship of Bible study, worship, Christian recreation and outreach." Training in "giving evidence of faith in Jesus through evangelism and discipleship" is a high priority, along with "encouraging a positive self-concept through Christian principles." Junior-high and high-school young people participate in a variety of activities as revealed in a sampling from the 1995 annual report:

1. Attending the annual Martin Luther King, Jr., Youth Rally in Phoenix.
2. Attending the "Boyz to Men" workshop and luncheon.
3. Teen Voice/Teens for Abstinence.
4. Attending an American Baptist Churches youth rally.
5. Visiting the Jewish Temple Beth Shalom for a worship service.
6. Sponsoring the "3-on-3 Hoop Jam."

Young adults are offered Friday night Bible Study, a "Marriage Boosters Workshop," participation in the annual Christmas program, attendance at the National Baptist College Age Fellowship in Memphis, Tennessee, and "Footstep," FIBC's dance ministry.

## Finance and Administration

Lemuel D. Cannon, formerly a financial officer with US West, is FIBC's minister of administration and development. Like most administrators in his position, he coordinates budget development with each ministry head. He presents a "budget package" to the trustees, ministers, and senior pastor for discussion and suggestions. He then sits with the budget and finance committee of the church trustees, reviewing the proposed budget in detail and emerging with a finalized budget for the year.

For Cannon, stewardship at FIBC has included a growth in tithing, but extends beyond financial giving:

We have truly become a church that has extended beyond the walls, the physical walls. I've been a member here since 1970. Basically, I remember [church] was just pretty much our Sunday, and we didn't have anything. Now we're a seven-day-a-week church. This building is in use every day, this educational facility. Some days we have to turn people down because we can't accommodate a meeting. But we're usually booked up. Next week, Monday through Friday, the Maricopa County Nurses Association has their annual meeting here. They'll be using all 24 of our classrooms and other meeting rooms. They would have paid from $5,000 to $7,000 at a hotel in Phoenix. When I talked with them, I said, "I'm not going to charge you $5,000. But I think you can pay $1,000 to help us keep the air-conditioning going!" So the word is getting out.

Cannon works with the pastor to make sure that the financial report distributed at worship services on the first Sunday of the month says exactly how much is given for Funds for Mission, and what specific causes were supported.

People can see exactly what happens with their money, how much is in our property expansion fund, what our general plans are, etc. We also publish a tithing chart. It doesn't say you have to follow it, but it says what you would be giving, if you tithed, for different income levels. It's not pushed down anyone's throat. It's a subtle reminder of what you should do.

Numbers come easily to Lemuel Cannon. Of the church's 2,600 members, Cannon estimates the "active number" at about 1,500, with an average Sunday attendance around 1,100. The 1997 annual report sent to me two years later made clear why FIBC can afford to be one of the largest givers nationally to both the American Baptist Churches' and the National Baptist (U.S.A., Inc.) Convention's mission funds. FIBC's total actual income for 1997 was $1,430,011.85, of which an astounding $1,161,663.17 came from tithing revenues. These figures mean an overall giving level of $550 per person in this 2,600-member congregation—but on the assumption of 1,000 households or giving units (probably a generous estimate), FIBC's average per-unit giving is closer to an impressive $1,430. Obviously, that average is, in a sense, an abstraction: the 20 percent of giving units that tithe contribute an extraordinary share of overall church revenues.

## Reflection: An Energetic Church of Prayer

Emblazoned on several programs and handouts I received at FIBC were the following:

*1996 Theme:* "Harboring Hope Amidst Hopelessness Under the Headship of Christ."

*Our Vision:* "Becoming an Evangelizing Fellowship Through Evangelism and Emancipation."

*Purpose:* "We are members of the body of Christ, believing and living, going and growing, sharing and caring as an active witness of the Kingdom of God on Earth."

It was a moving experience to hear the entire congregation at the 7:45 Sunday worship service recite the purpose statement together. What these members affirm out loud, what they as a congregation seem to be doing, what their leadership holds out as a vision and urges them to accomplish, appear truly to reflect the theme, vision, and purpose for which this church stands. In this respect, it vitally represents what Hadaway and Roozen mean by a growing church. I was struck by the "ing" verb forms in the purpose statement: they convey the ongoing dynamism of a congregation on the move, with evangelical reach to the community, caring about young people, raising its vision worldwide through its international prayer focus and its mission fund. Stewardship in every dimension seems to find re-markable fulfillment at First Institutional Baptist Church.

There seems to be no room in this church for anything resembling a passive stance. At a Sunday morning worship service, which indeed gave forth Hadaway and Roozen's sense of excitement and expectancy, the scrip-tural passage for the day was not read to the congregation by the pastor or a deacon. Instead the congregation joined in reciting it line by line. Next, I found myself picking up a pencil in the pew like everyone around me. The sermon was about to begin. Worshippers were turning to the page in the program titled "Listening to the Sermon." Underneath were the words, "Lis-ten to the message from God's Word. Use this sheet to make some per-sonal notes. Go back over them through the coming week. Let God crystal-lize His Truths in your life." Following were single lines each for "Sermon

Title," "Scriptural Text," and "Main Ideas of the Sermon." Blank lines then invited worshippers to jot down their reflections. At page's end were "Illustration I Want to Remember" and "What Should I Do as a Result of Hearing the Sermon?"

I mention this detail because it forms one more powerful indication that FIBC has virtually all the earmarks of a so-called "strict church." As economist Laurence Iannacone remarks, such churches have to hit an optimal level of strictness: Demands perceived by members as excessive will scare off potential new members; making too few demands risks the free-rider effect that reduces commitment and leaves members wondering what the group has to offer.[1]

First Institutional Baptist has managed to assemble a formidable array of commitment mechanisms that help bind members to the church and bestow a sense of good fortune to belong to it. My own view is that the pervasive emphasis on prayer is foremost among the "mechanisms" that act to spur members on, to deepen their commitments and mobilize their imaginations and their energies. From this emphasis, reinforced by the strong leadership of Pastor Warren Stewart, I believe, flow the energies that result in an impressive array of ministries and mission causes, plus an outreach to youth, as well as support groups addressing healing and other needs of members and the wider community. Stewardship is a pervasive dynamic at this church, evincing a strong sense of gifts given by God and to be returned to him.

## CHAPTER 6

# BUILDING STEWARDSHIP
# AMID YANKEE FRUGALITY

*All Saints Episcopal Church, Wolfeboro, New Hampshire*

On the drive from Concord to Wolfeboro, I murmured appreciation of the August landscape of New Hampshire, contrasting it with the sparse desert of my home state, New Mexico. Not having done my geography homework, I was quite unprepared for the stunning expanse of lake that suddenly came into view as we turned into Wolfeboro. It took a postcard purchased at the motel to tell me that Lake Winnipesaukee's 72 square miles make it the sixth-largest lake entirely within the United States.

Wolfeboro claims to be "the oldest summer resort in America," thanks to the last royal colonial governor of New Hampshire, John Wentworth, who built a summer home in 1763 on a lakeside hollow later christened Lake Wentworth. It isn't hard to understand why his wife wrote, "Wolfeboro is the place to recover appetites and learn people to relish what is set before them."

The first Episcopal services in the town were held in Governor Wentworth's home, a practice ended by the American Revolution a few years later. The Episcopal Church remained absent until 1888, when worship services were resumed by a neighboring pastor at Sanbornville. Not until 1944 was the first parish-owned building purchased. That year, All Saints Episcopal Church was admitted as a mission under the bishop of the local diocese.

The Rev. Randolph K. Dales became rector in 1978 and has seen a steady expansion in ministry and in hospitality to a wide variety of community groups in this vacation and second-home resort of 5,500 inhabitants. The parish evangelism statement echoes this development:

> As members of the body of Christ we witness our faith throughout the greater community. We do this in part by seeing and welcoming

newcomers to our church; by opening our church facility to the many groups which meet in our building each week; by aiding the less fortunate in our area through voluntary services to community groups. New members are sometimes brought into the church as a result of these activities.

A long list follows, from support groups to literacy and art classes to well-child clinics, outreach luncheons for seniors, the Wolfeboro Garden Club, Village Players. A longer list includes community organizations and institutions in which "many individual parishioners present a powerful Christian witness that is felt and valued in many places."

## Stewardship Perspectives

Father Dales saw even greater possibilities if only a more explicit stewardship base could be developed for what the congregation was doing. In 1995 he attended a national workshop sponsored by the Episcopal Church. The Rev. Hugh Magers, national stewardship director for the church, helped inspire Randy Dales "to begin to employ some of the things I learned there." Among them was to think of stewardship as a response of thankfulness to God rather than as a fund-raising effort. He is clear about stewardship goals for the parish:

> We're talking about a conversion of hearts that one would hope would lead to better support of ministries, both individually and collectively, as well as better financial commitment.

Dales knows how the word stewardship strikes many church members. "People will back up and hold on to their wallets. Sort of cringe." He tells the story of the Frankish king in the Middle Ages who, once converted to Christianity, decided to have all his army baptized:

> He marched them into the water, but some soldiers kept their right arm, their swords out of the water, so their swords wouldn't be baptized. I think Episcopalians have done that with their pocketbooks. It really comes out in the every-member canvass where somebody knocks on your door. People are uncomfortable doing

it and people are uncomfortable experiencing it. So when somebody says "stewardship" or "every-member canvass" or "fall loyalty"–whatever the code word may be–the immediate picture is, "Oh my God, somebody's going to come to my house and shame me into signing a pledge card!"

Dales hopes, of course, that a stewardship perspective will diminish these misgivings. But he also knows that while some parishioners "are joyful givers who themselves believe in the mission of the church and are willing to be involved with their bodies and their time," others are slower to respond.

"I want to see exactly where we're going before I join that program," or "I want to see where the money is spent before I contribute." That all comes out of either distrust in institutions, of churches, or of areas of control beyond the local–how much of my money is going into those national church things. There's a good deal of all of this.

*Would you say that it's easier, then, to preach giving of time and talent?*

It's probably easier, it's heard easier, when you talk about time and talent. That's controllable for someone. They know exactly what their efforts are going into. But they may not know where the money goes. But usually, when you start talking about giving of time and talent, people are waiting for the other shoe to drop. There's a reluctance–in the Episcopal Church, there's a reluctance to talk about evangelism. In another sense, we really are equally distrustful of talking about stewardship, because that's a little too scary a concept for a lot of people.

*Given what you've just said, how do you approach pledging, tithing, proportionate giving?*

Pledging has always been there. I've been trying to say to people that to understand yourself as a member of the church, you are pledging a commitment of yourself, part of which is the pledge. Now, not everybody gets the picture. Not everybody senses the

equation between being a member and being one who pledges. I
have talked a lot in specific sermons about financial giving, about
proportionate giving, as ways to set a measure for ourselves, or as
a goal. I have used the biblical tithe as the standard and talk about
the Episcopal Church statement on stewardship, which says that
tithing is the minimum standard. This theme is mentioned in our
parish stewardship statement, which has been reaffirmed by a
number of vestries, signed by most members as a commitment to
work toward the biblical tithe.

Randy Dales is referring to a statement in use at All Saints for several
years. Each group of new vestry members is asked to consider the statement and, if it meets the members' approval, to endorse it. I sat with vestry
members during my visit as new members scanned the statement (see below). No one objected. Several expressed appreciation for the notion of
proportionality, noting that when families hit hard times, they need not be
ashamed to reduce their giving. Others nodded approval to the practice
whereby 5 percent of one's income goes to the parish and 5 percent to
community charities like United Way or to more specific groups or causes.
Several responded positively to the ideal of remembering the church in their
wills and bequests.

The complete statement says:

We believe that stewardship is essential to the practice of Christianity, and we define stewardship to mean the giving of one's time
and money and talents to the glory of God in proportion to the gifts
God has given to us. As well, we affirm the Biblical tithe as the
standard of Christian giving of time and money. By this, we mean
the giving of at least ten percent of our time, as well as ten percent
of our income, for the work of God and for the spread of his
kingdom within as well as outside the church. We affirm the principle that the tithe includes giving time and money not only for the
support of the church, but also for the support of those in need
either through charities or individually, as well as the support of
our community.

To this end, we the elected leadership of All Saints Episcopal
Church declare that: a) we now tithe; or b) we pledge ourselves to
a personal program of increasing our giving of time and money
until we meet the goal of the Biblical tithe.

In addition, as stewards of our accumulated assets, we have executed, or will within this year execute wills, making arrangements for the disposal of our temporal goods, not neglecting, if we are able, to leave bequests for religious and charitable purposes.

We urge your prayerful consideration in joining us in this kind of commitment to Our Lord Jesus Christ and to the work of the Church.

*Do you let parishioners know about your own tithe?*

I tell them exactly what I do in terms of my own giving, where it comes out in terms of percentages, so they know what I'm doing. I find, as a clergyperson, though, that I'm reluctant to toot my own horn. It's trying to find a way between making an open witness and sounding like I'm better than thou. You have to couple that with the fact that a number of people perceive the budget as strongly driven by the cost of having a resident, full-time clergyperson. I'm also perceived, at times, as trying to raise my own salary. So that makes it a little bit difficult. I find a stronger witness is provided when I can get laypeople to talk about their own giving, to talk about the tithe.

Randy Dales gave me a copy of two such stewardship addresses from late 1994—common, of course, in many churches where lay members give witness just before fall pledging or giving drives. The first witness made a distinction between "up-fronters" and "rear-enders," characterizing himself as a "rear-ender for years." Following "prayerful consideration," he and his wife decided to begin each month "by writing a check for stewardship first and rely on what was left to cover our family's expenses" (a practice often referred to as "first fruits"). As in many such witness accounts, he affirmed that "we didn't lose our home, miss any meals, or go without any real needs," even discovering that they were able "to begin saving and investing for the future."

The follow-up witness by Senior Warden Cate McMahon focused more on the concrete needs of the church, pointing out that "our present level of pledging is not adequate to meet our operating costs," since only two-thirds of income comes from pledges. The shortfall was made up by the

"Lord and Tailor Thrift Shop" the parish operates, and by the summer fair. The fair is a major event at All Saints, a combination summer festival and auction that draws people from all of Wolfeboro and beyond. In 1995, it brought in $10,124; by 1998 its revenues rose to $14,606. This is no small contribution to a parish whose total income receipts were $133,225 in 1998.

> If we wish to expand our programs to include a Christian education person (which means adding another part-time person to our payroll), and to begin to do some of the programs we envision for the future, we will need more resources. We have just been given some wonderful insight into reviewing our personal commitment to see if it truly reflects our thanksgiving. We on the vestry and the rector have pledged ourselves to work toward achieving the biblical tithe.

At this point, the senior warden read the stewardship statement cited above. She concluded by suggesting that "if we give to God first, somehow everything else seems to fall in place," and by urging "each of you to seriously reflect on returning to God as a form of thanksgiving a portion of the many blessings he has given to us." In this way, she believed, "we can be assured that the All Saints parish that was established here 50 years ago will continue to grow and expand its outreach."

What I find interesting in this dual lay witness is that it combines two elements that virtually every pastor embracing stewardship finds essential: (1) an enunciation of the scripturally based biblical ideal, together with how this works out in the family of the witness, and (2) an explanation in concrete terms of what is needed by the parish, where the budget shortfall is, and what it takes to support new programs and agreed-upon ministries. Listening to Randy Dales reflect on his own theology of giving helps one to understand how a pastor can create a congregational climate receptive to the witnessing cited above. I asked him how he preached on stewardship, particularly given the challenge of doing so without suggesting to parishioners that God will reward them for increasing their giving:

> When people who tithe talk about the joys of giving and how much they get back from God, I think what they're trying to describe is the freedom and the joy that they've recognized in not

being enslaved by the things that they have. And I try to define that in a positive way without setting up a rewards-and-punishment scheme. I'm not very good on Boy Scout merit theology, but since I've always preached that God loves us where we are, who we are, which frees us up to do things, I've always talked about our giving as a return of what has been given to us—what is really not ours. And that runs counter to the message that secular society is telling us about having it all—it's yours, you earned it, don't let somebody take it away.

*Do you favor listing donors or pledgers, especially if someone has been especially generous?*

No, we don't have any plaques for any gifts given to the church, not since I've been here. Things that say, "Given to the glory of God" and, by the way, this is the person who gave it—seems like the first part of that sentence gets lost. I've been reluctant to take that approach—that is, making a list of "the sanctified" who are there. I find that really doesn't do a whole lot for the donors and kind of lays a guilt trip on others. I'm not sure it sets the example.

*How long do you think it will take to get the stewardship program you hope for up and running?*

Well, covertly we've been at it for a year and a half. More overtly now, just this year. I would say it's at least four years down the road to see some long-range impact. But I'm also doing things on a diocesan level to try to make a broader base of that. Everything that happens in the diocese this year on a major level—our diocesan convention, our fall clergy conference, all our diocesan council's yearly retreats—have stewardship and evangelism as primary themes, hand in hand. It's going to take a long time. I'm not sure, given the uniqueness of New England, whether it's ever going to be a done deal.

When I asked Dales about "the uniqueness of New England," he handed me copies of an article and an accompanying editorial in the *Concord Monitor*. A 1993 study commissioned by the New Hampshire Charitable

Foundation found that New Hampshire ranks lowest of the 50 states in per-capita charitable giving, whether compared in dollar amounts or in percentage of income. As the article commented, a regional effect seems to be in play: "There does appear to be a Yankee frugality . . . five of the six New England states occupy five of the bottom six rankings for charitable giving. Connecticut was the exception, ranking 36."[1] The writers seemed tentative and understandably embarrassed in trying to explain this pattern.

Stewardship, then, is a bit of an uphill challenge at All Saints, but to be fair, it is a recent emphasis, as Dales makes clear. He would like to see giving raised to the point of not needing separate fund drives, a desire expressed by many stewardship-minded pastors.

> Our giving isn't quite at that level as yet, so we have expanded the church plant, we have put in a "handicapped" elevator, and all of those were at such a significant financial level that they could not come out of just weekly offerings.

Around half of the parish's 260 households pledge. As for weekly offerings, Dales believes that while giving has gone up since he has been rector, "I don't think we're showing any great boost in the last year or so. It's really too early so say whether what we're doing right now has yet shown a great increase." A projected 1996 budget listed a total of $92,000 in pledges and plate offerings. Assuming 260 households in the parish, this means approximately $354 per household per year (this does not include Christmas and Easter offerings or fund-raising events during the year).

All Saints is also blessed with a modest endowment that includes a money-market account, a New Hampshire community loan fund, a consolidated investment trust, and a growth fund consisting of various securities. Their total worth at the end of 1998 was $206,226.

While Randy Dales was uncertain in 1996 about future revenues, by 1998 he had reason for optimism. The number of pledging units had risen steadily each year, from 105 in 1995 to 122 in 1998. The average pledge per unit increased from $759 to $832, with total dollars pledged rising from $80,737 in 1995 to $101,404 in 1998, an impressive 26 percent increase in three years. Clearly, the parish financial stewardship effort was enjoying success, which carried over into a creative stewardship initiative in 1998. He wrote:

This year for Stewardship Sunday when we passed out pledge cards, we changed our usual format completely. We held one service at 9 A.M.. (not two) and invited people to come in work clothes. We had lined up a number of cleaning and fix-up chores with leaders and supplies provided. We began the day with a short communion service and a sermon stressing that "this is our stewardship of what God has given to us; our work this day is a symbol and sacramental representation of what our money giving is all about." We gave people pledge cards, but also mops and paintbrushes! It turned into a wonderful day, the most popular activity being the multigenerational painting of the new fence for the nursery school. We continue to affirm one another's gifts and ministries.

In a conversation with two women who have been All Saints members for years (one a former vestry member, the other currently serving), it was apparent that All Saints takes imaginative approaches to fund-raising. Both commented with amusement on the success of the "Don't bury your talent" drive. Everyone in the parish was given a dollar and asked to see how much he or she "could make it grow." One of the women bought ingredients for and baked chocolate-chip cookies, which her husband promptly sold to students at a private academy where he taught. "I made 60 or 70 dollars on that one." Another parishioner used the dollar to print up notices and catered a party.

It was the only time I've ever seen an approach that included everybody, that made no distinction between people with literally the widow's mite and those with millions. The same, at least to start with. Everyone returned at least an extra dollar. It really drew people together, too, a dramatic way of encouraging people.

Both remarked that active volunteering in the parish reflects in part the large number of retired people in the church. "Except for the Sunday school and the fair, the younger people in the church really don't have the time to volunteer a lot of hours."

The two women were high in praise for the pastor's key emphases in his sermons. One remarked:

He once said that every preacher has one sermon that he just revises every so many Sundays. And his main theme is that we are loved. Randy preaches a great deal about [the idea that] because we are loved and cared for, it is critical that we must love and care for one another. If there's a message that consistently runs through his sermons, it is about caring for one another.

The other woman acknowledged that the rector encourages people "to support works like Hospice and Habitat, National Public Radio, whatever you think is important. Randy thinks that these kinds of concerns are definitely part of your tithing." Most families can give only so much, she insisted, "and if you're giving 10 percent to the church, then you can't give another 5 percent to these other causes. You have to balance this out."

All Saints prizes its invitations to all members to contribute. The annual parish meeting in the fall is generally a time for reviewing reports and electing new lay leaders. The 1998 meeting added a new item: Ballots were counted in which parishioners had prioritized choices from among "eight long-overdue capital improvements drawn from a lists of 106 projects submitted by parishioners." Projects ran from repairing the church steeple to a new sound system and new chairs for the undercroft, plus a new sign in the front of the church. Afterward, the rector honored 14 parishioners with "Almost Invisible Hands" awards, detailing the contributions of each of the honorees. If stewardship bestows a sense of ownership on church members, All Saints had managed, it seems, to embody that ideal in concrete fashion.

Community prayer finds expression in the Anglican tradition of the Daily Office of Evening Prayer celebrated during Lent. This prayer service of about 20 minutes takes place Monday through Friday evenings and is led by members of the parish.

As central as prayer is to this Episcopal community, its outreach in the broader community is no less vital.

## Ministries and Outreach

All Saints is justly proud of the high level of church and community involvement by its members. As I've already indicated, members are listened to and their suggestions often accepted. In response to a questionnaire sent to all families with school-age children, parents asked for more participation by their youngsters in the church's worship. They also voiced an expectation that their children receive a firm grounding in the Bible. Randy Dales's wife, Lynn Tyler, directs All Saints' church school. By 1998, 54 young people were attending regularly during the week in late afternoons and evenings. Classes range from preschool and kindergarten through middle-school children. The school adopted a new curriculum in 1998, basing each week's lessons and activities on the Sunday lectionary. "The Whole People of God" program provides stories, games, hands-on activities, and "intergenerational opportunities." A nursery school began in 1997, with the parish putting $17,000 of donations into fire-safety improvements and start-up costs. A year later the school was self-sufficient. After a beginning enrollment of 14 children, the 1998-99 school year saw 26 children enrolled. Parish volunteers staff the school, characterized in the 1998 annual report as "an outreach and fellowship to children and parents in our community. Our payment method and scholarship fund has allowed families of all incomes to be part of our program."

Boys and girls each have choirs in addition to the adult choir. Both altar guild and flower guild contribute to enhancement of Sunday services and provide additional service and special decorations at Christmas, Easter, Pentecost, and Thanksgiving. In a rural community of "you can't get there from here," the parish Caregivers program provides transportation primarily for senior citizens, mostly for medical needs. Low-income people also find transportation through this program to such destinations as well-child and WIC (Women, Infants, and Children) clinics. Fellowship and service activities are provided by the Episcopal Church Women (ECW).

Perhaps unique to the parish is the Lord and Tailor Thrift Shop. In the words of the 1995 annual report, "each Tuesday morning about six or seven devoted ladies meet to sort the donated clothing and other items." Half-price and dollar-day sales help to augment parish income (by approximately $9,000 in 1995). Clothing from the shop is also donated to a variety of groups, including Native Americans in North Dakota and needy families in the local community.

As mentioned earlier, All Saints also prides itself on member representation throughout the Wolfeboro community, whether it be in a hospice program (begun by the parish), prison ministry, LIFE Ministries Food Pantry, the Appalachian Mountain Teen Project, Carroll County Against Domestic Violence and Rape, Meals on Wheels, the Wolfeboro Public Library, a program to provide toys for prisoners' children, and many more. In 1998, the parish worked with the local Rotary Club to start a community youth center. It also raised over $4,200 to support hurricane-relief efforts in Honduras. A canvass of volunteer hours in 1995 produced a total of over 20,000, impressive for any church but particularly for a congregation this size, whose average Sunday worship service brings in 140 (not counting summer visitors).

## Reflection: Changing Stewardship Attitudes

All Saints Episcopal Church already had much going for it before the present rector introduced a stewardship emphasis: a lively outreach and welcoming stance toward the local community, involvement of members in a wide range of civic organizations and programs, and a pastor highly respected, even beloved by many of his parishioners. Its worship services were graced by participation of an adult choir plus boy and girl choirs; altar and flower guilds helped ensure that services were conducted in an atmosphere of beauty and dignity. My interviews with lay members assured me that members loved the church and what it stands for.

Aware of "Yankee frugality," Father Randy Dales believed that stronger congregational support could be generated through a stewardship approach; he attended a national conference devoted to stewardship formation. Fully aware of the resistance of many Episcopalians to talking about money, Dales has proceeded resolutely, confident that the involvement of so many of his parishioners in expressions of time and talent would also augur well for financial stewardship.

Dales exemplifies the ideal of a pastor willing to work with lay leadership in revisiting the identity and purpose of the church. A key strategy has been to ask vestry members to commit themselves to stewardship ideals contained in the stewardship statement, ideals that embrace tithing or working toward it and even encouraging the assigning of wills and bequests to the church and its missions. This top leadership commitment, together with lay witnessing, seems an excellent way to prompt consideration of stewardship ideals on the part of church members. Dales knows this endeavor will take years to achieve fruition, particularly because the parish is not exempt from the "regional effect" of low charitable giving that seems to characterize New Hampshire and neighboring states. His own stewardship preaching is marked by a positive emphasis on "God loving us where we are" and "As we give, we are free to do things." That approach and his articulating the seduction of secular society that "we can have it all" have combined to launch a dynamic stewardship approach at All Saints.

In a pattern visible in other stewardship-oriented churches, lay members are aware of two things: (1) They have long-standing giving habits to charities outside the church and are unwilling to increase their church giving at the expense of these favored charities. Thus the "five and five" approach in which the church receives "half a tithe" and community charities the other half, finds favor with many. (2) It is hard to expect people to look kindly upon increasing pledges and plate offerings on the heels of a capital campaign that has asked a lot from them.

An implicit dilemma arises here, because many experienced pastors and church-growth consultants hold that capital campaigns are excellent "lead-ins" to talk about increased regular church giving, often in a context of "so we don't have to go through building campaign after building campaign." The problem, of course, is that increased regular giving through pledges and more generous plate offerings takes years to build up. And in the meantime, the church roof needs replacing. Awareness of this dilemma prompts many pastors to focus principally on stewardship's promise of changing people's attitudes about money and riches, hoping these very changes will bear spiritual and material fruit in years to come. By late 1998, attitude changes had yielded a 26 percent increase over three years in both pledge dollars and overall revenues. Parishioner time and talent were being invested in expanding ministries. Stewardship ideals, it appears, had begun to bear fruit in tangible ways.

## CHAPTER 7

# STEWARDSHIP OF THE WORLD, NOT JUST OF OUR MONEY

*All Saints Church (Episcopal), Pasadena, California*

"You know, of course, that you're about to visit one of the flagship parishes of the Episcopal Church in the United States." My Episcopal friend was fairly close to the mark: I knew All Saints, Pasadena, was big, with a reputation for taking strong social-justice stands. That was about it. While waiting in the vestibule of a bustling main office for my first interview, I picked up a yearly report. All Saints' projected budget for 1997 topped $3 million, with $2.5 million coming from pledges (as that year ended, a successful "1997 Initiative" debt-reduction/deferred-maintenance campaign had raised an *additional* $2.5 million). More than 1,300 pledges were received, with the average pledge coming to $2,071. A long list of ministries followed. One, an after-school enrichment program for "children who are underserved" in the Pasadena community, was featured on ABC's "World News Tonight with Peter Jennings" in early 1997. A few months later, the *Wall Street Journal* carried an article on another of All Saints' financial success stories: the number of gifts of stock to the church more than tripled in 1997. No wonder the rector, who arrived in 1995, could write at the conclusion of his "State of the Parish" report in early 1998, "I am pleased, proud, and honored to be the Rector of this magnificent enterprise, ever stretching, ever searching for ways to be more nearly the people God is calling us to be." I very much looked forward to meeting the "CEO" of this "enterprise."

## An Interview with Ed Bacon

No pastor had ever objected to the word "invitation" in the definition of stewardship I presented in beginning an interview ("an invitation to members of a congregation to commit resources of time, talent, and money"). No one, that is, until I met the Rev. J. Edwin Bacon, rector of All Saints Church. "A weak word," he interjected, "in terms of what we do here." It was clear I was talking to a decisive man endowed with all the gifts of strong leadership. He launched immediately into four values of stewardship as presented and striven for at All Saints.

> It's really more a challenge than an invitation. The challenge is understanding primarily everything we have is a gift; even our breath is a gift. And so what we do with those gifts and how they become increased in our lives are primarily a result of our giftedness from God. Our act of thanksgiving is really to God for that giftedness. So that's one principle or value.
>
> The second has to do with our responsibility for stewardship of the world, not just of our money. Not just of our body, not just of our relationships, not just of our church. But of the world. And that's kind of a distinctive edge, I think, that we promote here: that the church really is secondary to concerns about knowing God–and working for the reign of God to spread. And that's going to take resources. And God is calling us to be God's people in the world to spread the reign of God.

*And that means caring for that world.*

> It's caring for the world, yes; but for us, it's also sharpened not only by the word "care," but by the phrase "dismantling injustice." In order for people to thrive, all God's people to thrive–and those who aren't thriving because of the institutional and systemic and structural injustice in the world–we have a job on behalf of Jesus Christ to dismantle all those structures of injustice. We are called to enable all those people to thrive the way we're thriving. So, in addition to understanding that all is a gift and that calls for thanksgiving, there's the notion of stewardship of the world and spreading the word of God.
>
> Then comes the third value, that of tithing. That is understood, in my thinking, as a sign to ourselves and to God that all of our resources are going to be used for the spread of the reign of God. So it's not a matter of giving 10 percent to the church so I

can take 90 percent and do with it what I want. Rather, I give 10 percent to the church to remind me that the other 90 percent is to be spent on the reign of God also. This is done through my children's education, through cars and clothes and on and on.

Fourthly, stewardship has to do with the mission of the church, in keeping this church going. And that speaks to the place of fund-raising for the church in the lineup of priorities and values.

*So fund-raising is encased within this whole context you've just described?*

Correct. But it is the *fourth* of the four values I've just mentioned.

*Fund-raising is . . . ?*

Yes. It *is* a reality. We are raising funds for the work of this church in the world. But it is the last of the four values. The first is the giftedness; the second is stewardship of God's creation and dismantling injustice. The third has to do with tithing and the fourth with fund-raising.

*So much of stewardship literature sharply distinguishes between "mere fund-raising" with the implication of a secular context, and true stewardship.*

And I think that's a false dichotomy. And everybody in the pew here thinks it's a false dichotomy, too. People who are savvy businesspeople in the world think "true stewardship" in that narrow sense is an ethereal, theological category that doesn't make sense to them. They know that if stewardship campaign season isn't effective or successful, then you're going to have to cut salaries, to cut services and on and on, unless you can balance the budget.

*So they're alert to the immediate consequences of not making budget?*

So yes, the invitation is to the parish for the parish to commit resources of time and talent and money, yes, out of thankfulness;

out of a desire to return God's gifts, yes, in order to advance his Kingdom in their community and beyond, yes. It's an invitation to take part in a formalized program and may involve further invitations, yes.

*And pledging is very much a part of this?*

Crucial. Simple. We set aside a season to gather in pledges. We start in April planning the fall campaign. We have more than 200 people, all volunteers, in a division of labor in one way or another- all the way from communications, which develops the theme and literature and sound bites, down to the people who make the phone calls after the season is over to get those pledges from our people who haven't yet turned them in. And a lot of different tasks and roles that are quite unique to each task all the way through the process from April to January.

Father Bacon produced two of his October "stewardship sermons" for me, delivered in 1995 and 1996. I quote somewhat at length from one of them below because it conveys, as no summary description could, the boldness and fearlessness with which giving is urged and parishioners challenged in this parish. Few better indications could be adduced of the seriousness of commitment asked of members of All Saints.

Biblical imagery abounds with the reign of God prominent in both sermons. In each, Bacon tells the congregation a story of inviting 200 of the parish stewardship canvassers to his home over a period of three evenings. After hors d'oeuvres and beverages, a kind of "canvassing rehearsal" took place among the rector's guests:

We literally gave people their pledge cards, paired them with other parishioners, and told them to talk with each other about how much they were going to be pledging to All Saints this year, and how they could increase their giving. We had folks talking about where they are in the tithing journey and learned that some people are just beginning and some people are now triple-tithing. This is real-life experience. That is vision lived out. That is life fully alive. We gave them instructions to honor one another by asking the other to give more than ever before. We said, "It is an act of respect to ask someone to stretch-to stretch in their giving, to become more like God, to be more like the Sea of Galilee, to be fully alive."

You see, when someone understands her or his true identity to be that of the image of God–watch out, world! That person is going to change and that person's church, mosque, synagogue, or faith community is going to change, and the world is going to change because there is an amazing amount of energy, vitality, and vibrancy released into God's creation. And so these canvassers will be asking you to stretch in your giving this year. They will be blunt, and they will talk frankly about money. This is an adult church, a grown-up church where we take pride in talking candidly about money and other things that matter. Don't be offended when they ask for a certain amount. They are paying you a compliment. . . . And they will be asking you to consider a tithe.

Ed Bacon is not without expert help in church financing. Rick Nordin, All Saints' director of development, brings to bear his experience as a gift and endowment officer for the University of Southern California Medical School. He thinks in terms of three types of giving: for yearly operating budget, for capital campaigns, and for estate planning. He points to a core of approximately 120 wealthy parishioners who form a major donor group. Nordin thinks of them as playing a major role in "a 12-month development perspective." Instead of resorting to occasional capital campaigns, Nordin favors, over the longer run, approaching this core of parishioners not just in terms of pledging to this year's operating budget, but of considering estate planning and generous giving to a capital campaign for debt reduction. As I indicated in the introduction, both efforts met with strong success the next year (1997).

Nordin likes to think in terms of available human energy. If donors are hit hard in the spring for a capital campaign, expect less energy from them in the fall. To be avoided, then, is hitting the same donors hard in both spring and fall. Better is an approach that helps them decide upon ways of giving that call for their planning over a longer time period. The pastor has to keep this financial leadership core well informed about the budget, the near- and longer-term needs of the parish.

# A Church for Social Justice: Two Portraits

### The Current Rector's Vision

Challenging church members goes beyond financial support, of course. All Saints' reputation as a church that takes (at times) unpopular stands is widespread throughout southern California and beyond. I ventured to Father Bacon that a social-justice emphasis was bound to collide with the conservatism of many businesspeople in his congregation (Pasadena is scarcely an impoverished community!). At some point in the past, I thought, that challenge had to have been engaged. Bacon was quick to agree, pointing to his predecessor. The Rev. George Regas (see following section) had not hesitated in 1969 to take issue with President Nixon's assertion that "the jury is still out" on the rightness of the Vietnam War. "This present jury is in," Regas countered from the pulpit and proceeded to denounce the war as immoral and contrary to the Gospel. It was an episode I was to hear about from several others before my visit ended. Families and individuals left the parish and/or withdrew their money ("You could hear the click of heels as people got up from the pews and walked out"). The die was cast. Determined to stay were those committed to a peace-and-justice church. They increased their pledges; sympathetic new members joined the church. "A decisive battle" was Bacon's forthright description.

That engagement has never ceased at All Saints. Bacon is sure that the point of engagement occurs within every person of the kind I brought up: conservative businesspeople as quasi-archetypes of Christians disturbed by the application of the Gospel to concrete "justice issues" of the day. "Politics in the church" is a familiar and fundamental expression of their protest. It is no different today (or in 1996, when I interviewed Bacon):

> We continue to take progressive social stances. To stay current, the hottest issues we are facing right now have to do with same-sex blessings, with banning "Saturday night specials" and related city ordinances regarding land use so that people can't sell guns here. It includes being against Proposition 209, which tried to do away with affirmative action; it includes being in favor of a living wage. These are recent engagements for us. And my sense is, every conservative person has to deal with what we are doing. We just think—I certainly believe—the way to do these things is head-on,

with all the candor in the world. I mean from the pulpit, making a full confession of where we stand.

I wondered if his exhortations were met with equal candor by members of the congregation, who might say, "Wait a minute-I am with you on three of those but on the fourth, count me out."

> Not in every case, but in many cases, yes–even the chair of the peace and justice committee. I took a stand against the president's policy in the Persian Gulf this past fall. When bombing was threatened, [and] then Saddam Hussein withdrew, I said absolutely no more bombing threats; that's not the way to go. And the committee chair said no, he disagreed with me. He thought the president's strategy worked. But he increased his pledge. That's part of the ethos here.

*Respect is accorded for a principled stand?*

> Well, there are folks who are the center of the life of this place who will do anything they can to protect the freedom of that pulpit. Even if they disagree with what the preacher might say, what is more valuable is to keep that pulpit free. Let me expand: We have a couple here who tend to be quite conservative (and most of our people are Republicans). Well, this particular couple got quite exercised over the fact that we took a stand on Propositions 209 and 210–Affirmative Action and Living Wage. They had some difficulty, I think, and just because they knew what this place was when they joined it two years ago, [that] didn't mean they wouldn't continue to have those difficulties with some of our stances, yet they support this church.

*You're talking about willingness to engage in the struggle.*

> True. And we talk the words "struggle" and "stretch" an awful lot here. We say that it's a compliment to ask someone to struggle, and we've used those words primarily in our giving because our giving and pledging approach is quite confrontive. Each person is called upon by another person in the congregation who's been

trained and has been given this person's pledge of last year, *plus* a suggested pledge to ask them for. So we ask people to stretch, and we ask people to struggle, and we talk about a mature church where people are *asked* to stretch and struggle, not only about money, but about sex and about politics as well as about theology.

I wondered whether Father Bacon relied upon documents of the church to help support a position he knew would be controversial.

No. I give a context in terms of biblical material and the history and tradition of this particular faith community. I am not averse to these sources. There might be an allusion to a bishops' statement on this or that position. I try to invoke biblical, prophetic literature.

I remarked that All Saints was coming across to me as a church well, even sharply, defined. Bacon agreed wholeheartedly and extended the thought through the metaphors of business:

Sharply defined is correct. And I believe with all my heart that's how to keep a place healthy: keep its market clearly differentiated. We are trying to differentiate our market at every turn.

## The Vision of the Rev. George Regas

Just before I left All Saints, it was my good fortune to obtain an interview with the retired rector, whose name had been so frequently mentioned in a prophetic context—"the church's guiding spirit," as one staff member remarked. As we settled into comfortable chairs in his living room, I asked George Regas how he understood stewardship. His response revealed what I believe is one of the profoundest expressions of the stewardship ideal, including its links to social justice, to be found anywhere:

It's the treatment of all which one has been given, inherited, and experienced. How do you responsibly deal with the gifts of God's creation? That means trees and the atmosphere and the lakes and how one cares for one's body, for one's family. Stewardship is the treatment responsibly of the gifts of life. That has been my under-standing: All of life is a gift. Stewardship is one's response, one's use, of that gift. I think we make a mistake in *not* tying that to money, and we make a mistake in *only* tying it to money.

*So stewardship is not just fund-raising.*

No, no. What I tried to do is to combine stewardship and fund-raising, both unapologetically. You don't raise much money if you just do fund-raising and you don't raise much money if you just do stewardship. You have to combine them. I am talking about people becoming aware of the incredible blessings of God, that we are loved and given so much by God. Once people become sensitive to those gifts of grace, the thankful person responds with money. So stewardship embraces God's mercy and generosity but with thanksgiving as a motivation. On top of that, though, I preached and taught that we let all of this inform the environ-ment: We live in a grace-filled community, and we're thankful people. *Then* we bring to bear all the best understandings of fund-raising techniques. We go from there to suggested askings for people. We concentrate energies on the highest potential.

*In other words, don't sell people short.*

Exactly. But initially, people were distressed at the good-hearted secular techniques of fund-raising. Now, no university would think of doing a campaign without knowing that John Doe is going to be asked for "X" amount of money. The church community got apprehensive in the early days. By now, it's just part of our life at All Saints. As you know, we train callers to go into your home and say, "Patrick, would you be willing to consider next year making a pledge of $200 so we can move toward the goals we have?" In this process, we make sure we sit down with you and share the vision, share the hopes and dreams, and then ask you into those. Of course, we train the callers to share their stories: "This is what God has done in my life; this is what the church means to me. I'm here to share with you and ask you to consider joining some of us who are giving at this level."

*This is combining stewardship and fund-raising.*

Yes. And if you do one without the other, no matter which you choose, you're going to diminish both.

*What advice would you give a pastor inaugurating a stewardship approach, but just coming off a big capital campaign? "I don't want to exhaust my people by asking them to enhance their plate offerings at this time."*

I don't think there's ever a good time for a capital-fund drive, and there's never a good time to start stewardship. There's always stuff you could reasonably put on the table against them. I believe the community of faith needs to be part of the problem and part of the solving of problems. We're not trying to figure out a good time to finesse someone.

*Not a question of pastor versus people?*

No. Here it is: We've just raised a million dollars in this capital campaign, and yet we still have a ministry, and God calls us to do that ministry, and so let's talk about it. It's a partnership, a collaboration; it's the pastor *and* the board and the vestry, the session; they, we, all combine our efforts and our commitments. It's not the pastor doing it so much as the pastor asking the people to come into this thing. Let me say, though, that if the pastor is not a tither, no headway will be made. The pastor has to say, I am committed to tithing. Not in any bragging sense—just "This is where I am."

*But talking about money does raise anxieties.*

Few people ever get to the point where giving has no tension to it. There are a few saints in the world, but most people have that anxiety. I think you just create a church in which that struggle, that anxiety, is part of the culture of the church. It's not just something you do one year and it's over. Part of the total mission is to talk honestly about money, challenging people to come into a real engagement with the tithe. And that produces conflict and apprehension, but it puts people right at that point where God does great things in their lives. And once, as a pastor, you go through that anxiety and agony and conflict, you have put yourself in a place where the spirit really works, can get inside of people and begin to do marvelous things. So, stewardship, to be effective, is a stewardship revolution. It is big, potent stuff.

*And it is countercultural?*

Sure. The idea today is far more "What can I get for myself?" and how little I must put into the common pot. Heroic generosity, strong attachment to the common good more than individual wealth–those are countercultural positions. We live in an individualistic society. So when you say, I want to be generous so that the city can be healthy, so that the community can be healthy, so the nation–the world–can be healthy, that's moving against the tide.

*One pastor told me that Jesus speaks more about wealth and its uses and dangers that he does about prayer.*

No question about it. You hear pastors say, "I don't want to know what my people give." But giving is an index to a person's spiritual health–not in quantity terms, but in terms of its relationship to resources. If someone has lots of money and gives little, that says something. If a person has modest income and gives a lot, that says something about spiritual health and vitality.

*Let's turn to social-justice ministry. All Saints is a prophetic church. How did you come to the stands you took, like that on the Vietnam War? What about the effect on church membership?*

Some very conservative people of wealth in those days couldn't deal with all of that, and they left. But more people have come. But if a prophetic ministry is dogmatically superimposed on a congregation, you're in trouble: You won't have much of a congregation; you won't have much money. But if a congregation comes to participate in seeing that what God wants us to do with life is create a more just society, God wants us to deal with the homeless and those with AIDS, with violence, with sick children—that somehow our resources, influence, and power of our community can be brought to bear on issues that hurt human beings—a lot of people begin to hear, to listen. I think down deep, there is a goodness in people. When they see a community really at work, substantially improving the life of a community, many will say, if I'm going to be part of a church, I think this is what I want to be part of. Even if I don't agree with all they're doing, like gun control. But there's something in that place: they're trying their best to create the kind of world that Jesus would want us to have. More people say yes to that than say no. Think about it: All Saints has the most radical, most prophetic out-on-the-edges ministry of any church, and we raise more money.

*I'm struck, though, that so many of your parishioners are wealthy, they are contributors to conservative causes, to the Republican party—all that.*

But see, that's disregarding the basic goodness in people. That's thinking that down deep people aren't drawn to the work of healing. It *has* taken a lot of hard work. It just didn't happen overnight. A stewardship program isn't produced in a couple of weeks. Takes years. A huge amount of work and energy, a huge time commitment.

And a lot of patience, it seems to me.

And work. Take the new rector, Ed Bacon. He has to raise from people three million dollars in annual giving. The effort and prayer and collaboration, lay building and leadership training—all that is an enormous challenge. But the results are terrific.

See, the thing in stewardship—not only does the hard work produce the dollars to do important work; it produces the vitality to sustain it. Stewardship brings into a congregation incredible vitality and energy. Always to be stretching to make it. To be among the largest churches in the Episcopal communion and to know that the Sunday offering is necessary to pay the bills. It's that enormous kind of tension, that we operate this huge ministry based upon your generosity. It just does something to congregations.

George Regas was not impressed by personal spiritual development unconnected "to the totality of life." Saying you are into spiritual development may imply that "I'm not into all this activism stuff. I'm developing my soul."

There's nothing wrong with that except that your soul won't be developed much if it's not connected to politics and economics and sexuality and community. It's the totality of one's life that All Saints is trying to deal with. Money is part of that, and activism is part of that; worship is part of that. So is being alone and trying to listen to what God's saying to you—all that is part of it.

*I've heard it said: Build up ministries first and only subsequently talk about money.*

Yes and no. How do you get ministries going when you don't have money to pay anybody? Besides, that's separating the pastor from the people, separating decisions on what to do from what God is calling us to do. I think a pastor needs to get in there and say, "What are we about? Where is God asking us to have ministry?" Just in that question is, how do we pay for it, how sustain it? At All Saints we never talk about anything that's disconnected [from] the dollars. Everything that goes on in a parish is in some way related to dollars.

*You're stating a holistic vision.*

I think people need from the beginning to integrate money into total discipleship, integrate money into the total life of the Christian, into the total life of what this church is about. Would you wait until some appropriate time to talk about prayer, or to deal with the Bible, or with the sick? It's just part of the life we have been talking about.

*How did you come to the prophetic stance that characterized your leadership at All Saints?*

Well, I went to a liberal seminary. But I think I was predisposed to that. I was the son of a Greek immigrant who was always at work in the community, trying to give back. He was a good citizen, so I grew up in the environment. I grew up in the South during segregation. But there was a predisposition toward justice. Yet it was only as I listened to people where I was assigned to work that my mind and heart and spirit were shaped—and always in interplay with the community. Everything we've done at All Saints involves engagement of the pastor and the prophet with the community of prophethood.

It's a mistake to think the people are not shaping that. Everything we have done at All Saints has had my leadership, but sometimes that came after I'd been pushed and shoved by people who felt this is where we ought to be. Sometimes I pushed and shoved them; sometimes they, me. The key element is the interplay of people and pastor.

*I have to say that one of the outstanding characteristics of "stewardship pastors" I have been visiting is that they are not control freaks. They are eager to involve the congregation in goal-setting and decision-making.*

And the places that do nothing are those where the pastor says, well, they are so conservative and reactionary here that when I'm brave in my prophecy, I get into trouble. Well, people get in trouble when they're control freaks or when they can't love those who have a different view. That's where you get in trouble.

*I would love to have been in on the conversations you've had over the years with, say, wealthy bankers, etc. Those must have been real engagements!*

They were hard. Some I lost; some I didn't. But people want to be taken seriously. They want to be seen as trying to be a good Christian with the divergent view. And sometimes you don't make it. But most of the time, if you give that person respect and time to allow him or her to grow and use the good stuff inside that person, you will win more than you lose.

Prophetic ministry is hard; it takes time, energy, persistence. Prophetic ministry is not just popping off in the pulpit. All Saints is a church that has populated practically every committee in Pasadena that deals with justice issues. Everywhere you go you'll see All Saints people involved. These are people at work, finding nurture, finding leadership, finding direction, finding help from clergy.

*As the church engages public issues, though, it seems to me to run into that thin line between the prophetic and the really political, like gun control, perhaps.*

Where we make a mistake is to think that any aspect of life is nonpolitical. Jesus says, heal the sick. A predominant part of his ministry lay in healing. So he says, as the Father sent me, so I send you to be healers. But how can anyone today talk about healing nonpolitically? It is a public-policy issue, one determined in the state legislature and city council and in Congress. It's determined by how professions look at health and how much power government is allowing the HMOs to have, etc. Now to say that to be a healer, you have to support the Democratic version of this bill, that's crazy stuff. What *does* make sense is to say, we must get into the battle to influence public policies that will bring about the best health care to this poor person. Yes, it is all very complicated, but our task is to influence public policy and not to shy away from the complicatedness of it all.

Let me conclude by saying that to be partisan is unacceptable, but to be involved is the mandate we have. I'm very, very distressed with what is happening to welfare. We've got to bring judgment on that. We've got to challenge what it means to be the poorest of the poor, because that's our task in the church.

I believe that more money will come to the church if the church is significantly involved in creating a better society. But only if the church is willing to put the energy and the perseverance into holding on to that conviction and helping people to come along. You can't do it right away, but long term, the church that's going to survive is the church that people know is committed to the survival of our culture and of our society and of our children.

## All Saints' Mission Statement

I reproduce the essential elements of the mission statement, as handed to me by Father Bacon, because I believe it powerfully conveys the rationale and core spirit of the church today:

The first All Saints parishioners, 11 in all, gathered in 1882 in the living room of a small house tucked into a Southern California orchard. A century later, the Church had become the largest Episcopal congregation in the western United States and a national beacon for progressive Christianity. The Church celebrates a rich spiritual and liturgical life and its ministries reach far beyond the church walls. From its stands against the Vietnam War to its struggle against apartheid, All Saints has been in the vanguard in fighting for peace and justice at home and across the globe.

Blending the ritual beauty of classical Anglican tradition with contemporary expression of Jesus Christ's liberating love, the Church strives to live both individually and corporately in a vivid implementation of the gospel. At three Sunday worship services, All Saints welcomes each and every one of its 1,300 worshipers to the Eucharist, sending forth the congregation to live and serve with charity and devotion. Parishioners reach into almost every corner of community life. Church volunteers founded Union Station, a pioneering homeless shelter committed to rebuilding broken lives, and the AIDS Service Center, the San Gabriel Valley's largest resource for people affected by HIV and AIDS. Among the newer ministries are Young & Healthy, bringing medical care to uninsured children; EDEN, an environmental ministry; COLORS, which seeks to overcome racism; and Seeds of Hope, which places parishioners throughout the city tutoring children.

All Saints' commitment to change has transformed the liturgical experience as well. The staff and the congregation were among the first to push for the ordination of women and the blessing of same-gender covenants. Combining the best elements of high and low church, All Saints celebrates everything from the All Saints' Day Requiem with a chamber orchestra to rock masses with live bands.

The pulpit, which plays a central role in worship every week, has welcomed such diverse preachers as theologian Matthew Fox and Archbishop Desmond Tutu. The Church also leads a multidimensional Sunday education program, from classes for children to gatherings for adults. The Sunday Rector's Forum, a centerpiece of parish life, has welcomed political activist Daniel Ellsberg, television producer Norman Lear, and children's advocate Marian Wright Edelman, among many others.

The church is supported by the generous giving of 1,500 pledging units who are individually canvassed annually. The current operating budget of $3 million is among the largest in the national Episcopal Church.

## Planning Youth Ministry

The dynamism reflected in the statement above suggests a process whereby ministries are reviewed and new initiatives considered. Bacon told of two two-day retreats for himself and the management staff. Another two-day retreat brings together vestry members and rector. Planning takes place during these retreats. But this isn't all. George Regas had set up a program review committee that would focus each year on one program area. Ten people make up this committee. Youth ministry was the focus in 1995, resulting in a task force at work throughout 1996. Adult education received attention as well.

When I suggested that young people in their twenties were a concern for many denominations, since they seem anti-institutional and critical of existing forms of worship and moral stances, Bacon's demurral was revealing:

We're not concerned or anxious in the sense you're talking about. We *are* concerned in the sense of wondering what is going on because my assumption—and I think our assumption at All

Saints–is that the nature of faith will change and the nature of the church will change. Why be anxious about perpetuating what has served one generation when it may not serve the next? In order to service the next generation, the principle of incarnation is to find the new ways in which to make the faith relevant. Our question, then, is "What will it be?"–and let's go ahead and change.

Another concern would be, there's a wonderful debate going on in catechesis right now. A newer voice says [that] catechesis, correctly understood, is not indoctrinating somebody into your own language forms, but finding out from them how God is active in their lives, and then adapt those language forms. The Anglican Missionary Movement is our model for that, because we've discovered that in the traditional missionary model, when you go in and say, let us bring God to you, that would have failed. But when you go in and say, tell us how God is already here, and let us help you celebrate that–that has to be done with Generation X as much as it had to be done in the darkest of Africa in the thirties and forties.

*This would include music as well as speech.*

And worship materials, too. That's why we're asking our questions about liturgy and music for the 21st century. I have my eye on what Matthew Fox discovered in Sheffield, England. He found a commune of Christians in the Church of England pastored by a 24-year-old priest. They were doing what was colloquially called "a lay Mass." They would have it in a warehouse one night and a park the next and elsewhere the next night. It was technologically advanced, with a synthesizer and flashing lights and all the multimedia stuff–all trying to find new forms in which to communicate with kids. So we have to do the same process for the kids in Los Angeles who attend here.

## Adult Education

Lenten study groups organized around a "Lent Event" speaker are just one example of the stewardship of adult growth cherished by All Saints. Moreover, on any given Sunday morning between worship services, between 500 and 700 people are engaged in some form of adult education. Bible study, personal growth, and peace-and-justice classes are among the choices. Midweek offerings in 1997 included a study group on Mark's gospel and on the Acts of the Apostles. Occasional Saturday morning offerings included discussion groups on theology and the nature of God. The parish's Jesus scholar in residence was Scripture scholar Marcus Borg, who discussed his own theological reflections, "The God We Never Knew." The Lenten Series for 1999 begins with a keynote address by Old Testament scholar Walter Brueggeman. All Saints staff members offer follow-up discussion sessions. Other Lenten small-group meetings and midweek classes are also scheduled.

## Reflection: A Bold, Prophetic Vision

"Unapologetic leadership" offers a ready characterization of this church, but one fully understood only in historical context. When retired rector George Regas stated that his predecessor, in 1942, ascended the pulpit to denounce the removal of Japanese-Americans from their homes and their internment in camps, he was letting me know that All Saints stood in a long tradition defined through struggle by strong leaders with a prophetic vision. "This meant that I could do no less when it came to the bloodshed in Vietnam." Strong traditions in a vital organization carry leaders with them; leaders are, in a real sense, servants of those traditions and find they "can do no less."

This prophetic vision has come to define stewardship at All Saints. Although rector Ed Bacon did allude to raising funds for the church's ongoing mission and ministries, he described fund-raising as the *last* of the four values of stewardship at All Saints. Its stewardship theology comes first: We are all gifted and praise God in how we use these gifts out of thanksgiving for our giftedness. The second value, Ed Bacon insisted, articulates "the distinctive edge" of stewardship at All Saints: We are responsible for stewardship of the world, not just of our money. This care for the world extends to "dismantling injustice—we are called to enable all people to thrive the way we are thriving." Tithing, as the third value, is the call to use the resources we have been given for the spread of the reign of God. Giving the 10 percent is to serve as a reminder that the remaining 90 percent is also to be spent for the reign of God, but this ideal embraces our education, our homes, our vacations and so on—all gifts to be enjoyed as they fulfill us and further prepare us for extending God's reign outward (as I understand it) through concentric circles from individual and family to the outermost ring, the world itself.

Resistance to such a vision is fully expected at All Saints or anywhere else. Its leadership, beginning with the rector and extending through vicars and staff, vestry and committee chairs and members, has not hesitated to grapple—"wrestle" was George Regas's word—with this resistance. Money is talked about "up-front." It is not a topic to be avoided whenever possible because it might offend a lot of people. The yearly canvass involves members "giving respect" to those they approach by asking them to "stretch" in their giving, "to be fully alive." This is a highly intentional approach, running directly against the fear, widely cited in stewardship literature, of bringing up money. "We are paying you a compliment in asking you for money." I believe it takes little away from the commendable boldness of this approach to note that it is addressed to parishioners who are quite well off (and their numbers are large) and who are expected to lead the way in generous giving. They are the very members "of whom much is expected."

More important, experience with this "unapologetic leadership" has left All Saints' rectors and stewardship directors and committee members with a basic conviction: although direct challenge on social-justice issues will indeed upset some members, their basic allegiance to All Saints remains. The church's wide array of ministries that obviously serve those in need (e.g., tutoring disadvantaged students) offsets the misgivings prompted by prophetic ministry. This happens precisely because these members recognize and admire what the church is attempting and doing in the community, notwithstanding their disagreement on particular issues. This is unmistakably a church with an evangelistic outreach to the community that surrounds it. Moreover, many members will eventually be won over to the very social-justice causes and ministries that may have offended them in the first place. Undergirding these convictions is a basic refusal, in George Regas's phrase, "to disregard the basic goodness in people."

Finally, and by no means least, the care and striving for excellence that go into worship at All Saints—a splendid liturgy and superb music whose reputation extends far beyond All Saints' boundaries—in themselves convey the reassurance to those who need it that this is indeed a church of prayer, a conviction reinforced by the small-group ministries designed to help nourish parishioners' spiritual lives and to show the connection between the latter and one's call to further the reign of God through commitment to social justice.

Both rectors I spoke with expressed a conviction shared with others I interviewed: This is not a church for everyone. By no means all those seeking a house of worship will resonate positively with the messages coming from All Saints' pulpit. Supporting a ban on handguns in the local community will not strike everyone as what the church ought to be doing. But that's just the point: All Saints embraces—or is embraced by—a tradition of fearless proclamation of its vision of the Gospel, calling for commitment to dismantle injustice both distant and nearby and to give generously to support this commitment. Stewardship expands, under this vision, to embrace responsibility for the whole world, for people everywhere who are needy, hungry, thirsty, and without means, who are marginalized even within affluent societies. Such an understanding of stewardship takes a long, long time to nurture and make grow. This is not the driving vision of every church. But for those open, or opened, to its message, All Saints provides a compelling beacon on the hill.

## CHAPTER 8

# Spiritual Gifts:
# Finding How You're Wired
# Deep Down

*Northkirk Presbyterian Church, Alta Loma, California*

The smallest of all the churches in this study is located within a larger southern California suburb whose name older readers will recall as the butt of many jokes on the Jack Benny radio program, Rancho Cucamonga (population 115,000). With only 150 members in 1996, Northkirk Presbyterian Church in Alta Loma led all 35 churches in the Presbytery of Riverside in mission giving per member. "Humble beginnings" seems the right phrase. The Rev. Darel Griffin, associate pastor, put it graphically: "We got started in the high school and the music room, the boys' gym, the community service building." That was 1980. By the time I visited in November 1996, the congregation had purchased a vacated church building in 1993 and settled in comfortably. The pastor, the Rev. Dick Green, elaborated on stewardship from his office just outside the sanctuary:

> We try not to make stewardship just something we talk about in October, November, but as it comes up naturally in the course of the year. In talking about people using their talents, we bring up spiritual gifts and finding how you're wired deep down inside and how God has gifted you. We encourage people and try to help them discover what their giftedness is and how all that might coincide with ministries within the church and outside it. A lot of times people burn out because they're just plugged into the wrong ministry. Sure, they want to serve and they volunteer, but it may not be the ministry that fits who they are. So they get discouraged and burn out quicker than if the ministry really touches who they are.

How are spiritual gifts discerned? In Darel Griffin, Northkirk has the advantage of an experienced pastor who enjoys his volunteer role as Dick

Green's pastoral associate. Griffin and Elder Sandy Gabel conduct small-group classes on spiritual gifts based on the work of William Easum. A two-page handout, "Insights to Spiritual Gifts," serves as a guide. Scriptural references are listed under two major headings: "To Whom and How Are Spiritual Gifts Given?" and "What Is the Purpose of Spiritual Gifts?" Completing the handout are lists that contrast (1) talents with gifts and (2) the fruit of the Spirit with the gifts of the Spirit. A notable consequence is visible in Northkirk's "Ministry Opportunities" guide ("'Ministry' is anything you do for others for the glory of God"). Not surprising are listings under "Congregational Support Ministries" and "Outreach Ministries." A subsequent section, however, is titled "Spiritual Gifts and Ministry Match-Up." Ministries are regrouped according to spiritual gifts; e.g., leadership, hospitality, administration, discernment, music, craftsmanship, healing, giving, mercy, teaching, exhortation, intercession, prophecy, and evangelism, among others. Some ministries are found under two or more gifts. Pastor Green also preaches several times a year on spiritual gifts.

It would, I think, be difficult to find a more effective way of motivating church members toward ministry involvement. The high participation of Northkirk's members derives in no small measure from this effort. Darel Griffin does not hesitate to draw a contrast:

> My reading would say that often 10 percent of the church carries the remaining 90 percent. Well, here it's the opposite. Ninety percent, I would say, are active in ministry and are seriously concerned about their giving of time, talent, and money.

Dick Green put some numbers on Griffin's estimate.

> We recently counted people who did things in the church. Out of a hundred and fifty members, we had between a hundred and ten and a hundred and twenty members who were doing something. It might be a minimal involvement all the way up to a very committed type of ministry in the church. I think we're successful partly because we're smaller. The smaller you are, the more likely a higher percentage [are] involved in ministry.

Preparation for ministry occurs through a class taught by the church's evangelism committee. Darel Griffin also conducts a "Master's Plan" class that trains members for evangelism. But involvement doesn't happen just through sheer training. New-membership classes held two or three times a year are a vehicle for getting across what's expected:

> Our message is, "We hope you want to join the church. Membership means in part that you're going to help us reach our vision and mission. If you're not ready to do that, we understand. We still love you, we still want you to come, and we will minister to you, but when you're ready to take the step of membership, you're saying to us that I'm ready to do what I can to help Northkirk reach its mission and ministry goals." It's also at that time we begin to mention spiritual gifts and how they can match up with teaching or ushering or singing or whatever the ministry might be. That's a strong component of the new-members class.

*There's no such thing as a spectator member here?*

> Well, we do indicate that if you're not ready for that, OK, but being a member means being a participant, and we make that fairly clear.

Besides stepping into the pulpit in Pastor Green's absence, Griffin contributes impressively to Northkirk's "time and talent" dimension of stewardship. He meets weekly with a small Promise Keepers[1] support group, helps organize men's retreats through the "West End Cluster" of Presbyterian churches, and assists in putting together teams of would-be house-framers on behalf of Habitat for Humanity. He and his wife, Joretta, serve as part of a clergy team for Presbyterian Marriage Encounter weekends and together and have been designated "the Southwest Couple" on the National Board of Presbyterian Marriage Encounter. Not every small church has the luxury of a dedicated pastoral associate team. Northkirk is indeed fortunate.

While appreciating the Griffins' assistance, Green admitted that Northkirk "is a bit slim" on formally organized outreach ministries, but he was quick to list what church members were doing in the community:

> Several work at a place called "Santa Claus," where they receive used toys and repair broken ones to be given to needy families at

Christmas. Several work with food-distribution banks, including one sponsored by a local council of churches. A women's group here has gotten involved with the local crisis-pregnancy center, particularly a program where you adopt a young woman—that is, our members provide emotional support, and if they can help physically as well, they do so. We have others who read tapes for the blind. Hospice volunteers, too. Our own mission giving includes various feeding programs. Our deacons' fund supports needy persons in our congregation as well as people who just drop in. Our deacon training involves not just handing these persons a voucher or whatever, but actually praying with that person or meeting with him or her and getting a little more personally involved.

Ministries ideally grow "from the grass roots and not from the top down," Green affirms.

In fact, a lady called me today. Our women's group wants to do this Angel Tree Ministry, which is about gifts for children of prisoners. It was their idea, and I said sure. It excites me when individuals or groups come up with a ministry. They're trying to live out their Christian faith. As pastor, as staff, as session, we bless these things and help them go ahead and do it. Top-down means it's my idea or the session's. Then the question is: Who can we get to volunteer? I like to see it turned around where people say, "I've got this ministry idea, and two or three other people are willing." Then we'd say, "Well, how can we help you? How can we bless this?"

*You obviously feel more comfortable nurturing and encouraging rather than controlling.*

Yeah. I'm sure I have lapses at times, but I don't feel I have the need to control or be in charge of everything. I tend to do more than I should upon occasion. I believe as a pastor I should offer leadership and direction but not control.

Dick Green may feel he's "not in charge of everything," but when a particular education ministry appeals to him, he "engages." In the summer of 1997, he took charge of the "YONKS" (Youth of Northkirk) junior-high group. He leads them every Wednesday evening during the school year in fellowship, singing, games, and Bible study, assisted by an adult female member of Northkirk. During the summer, the group meets once a month for pool parties; the youth also enjoyed a rafting trip. In early 1998 the young people made a weekend retreat with Dick Green as one of their two counselors. Senior-high "YONKS" are led by four adult church members. Besides a summer retreat, they also attend a February winter camp. Senior-high students also undertake several service projects during the year. Younger children are served in Sunday school and on Friday nights. In 1998, Northkirk organized a chapter of the Pioneer Club, a midweek children's ministry that focuses on "Christ in Every Phase of Life." Green again took leadership by helping recruit teachers and staff. A director of this club was to be sought in 1999 to help expand events and activities.

Worship at Northkirk is graced by several choral groups. "Praise Singers" are heard at most Sunday worship services; "special choirs" perform during Lent and Advent. A children's choir is heard at Christmas. Northkirk also hosts two Friday evening gospel music concerts during the year, offering local Christian musicians a chance "to share their commitment to Christian music and offer alternative worship for the community" (1997 annual report).

Mission giving forms a central ministry in most Presbyterian churches. In 1998, officers and members of the mission and stewardship committees agreed to merge into one stewardship/mission committee for that year. An immediate challenge was not only to conduct the three familiar special offerings and mission campaigns—One Great Hour of Sharing, Peacemaking Offering campaign, and CROP Walk—but to refinance the existing building loan, taken out at time of construction several years ago. The Presbyterian Investment and Loan Program was the instrument chosen to effect the refinancing. This program asks the local church to provide loans from individual members to the program's own capital funds, which are then used to provide a continuing source of funds to other churches. As of December 1998, 27 individuals from Northkirk had invested a total of $176,750 in the program. If additional Northkirk members invest enough in the program to reach $185,000 in 1999, the church's interest rate will be reduced by one-quarter percent.

As mentioned earlier, Northkirk is number one in overall mission giving within the presbytery. Funds go also to "Amen Missions" to train missionaries in Peru. In addition, 10 percent of Northkirk's budget goes to general missions supported by the Presbyterian Church (U.S.A.) nationally. As is the case in many churches, visiting missionaries from around the world make their cases during visits to the congregation.

## Stewardship of Money

Dick Green does mention tithing in his sermons, but he prefers to emphasize proportional and sacrificial giving. When he does talk about tithing, "it's not as a legalism, but rather something you could shoot for and build towards over the years. Or even go beyond that if you are a tither because the New Testament puts no limits on our generosity." Green prefers to speak of stewardship "as a spiritual matter, expressing our relationship with God and a way of rendering our thanks for what God has done. And I think people are picking it up."

My November visit coincided with one of Dick Green's principal stewardship services. Distributed to everyone was a one-page sermon outline on which Green elaborated:

MOTIVES FOR GIVING
1. We give to needy people out of love.
2. Partnership in ministry.
3. Harvest ("As we sow, thus we reap").
4. The love of Christ Jesus ("Thanks be to God for his inexpressible gift").

CHARACTERISTICS OF GIVING
1. Generosity is a gift (chairs).
2. True giving is overflow ("from hearts warmed by God's love").
3. Christian giving must be sacrificial giving ("widow's mite–our gifts cannot be cheap").
4. Christian giving is eminently practical ("Needs must be met").

PRINCIPLES OF GIVING (Christians of Acts are models here.)
1. Their giving began with God's giving.
2. Their giving was stimulated by that of others.
3. Their giving to this collection came on top of regular giving.

4. It was a generous freewill offering ("because they wanted to").
5. It was their attitude that mattered to God ("no grumpy givers, but rather, as God has prospered us").
6. Their giving all sprang from self-giving ("They first gave of themselves, trusting that God will supply our needs").

RESULTS OF GIVING
1. Needs were met.
2. Their characters were refined ("they continued to grow").
3. They met needs and evoked thanks and prayer among God's people.
4. God was glorified ("others saw how Christians were giving to one another").
5. Finally, they became magnetized afresh by God's great gift.

Each point was made in Green's easy conversational style. He encouraged worshippers to take notes on the sermon following the outline on the handout. I noticed many around me doing just that.

The 1998 stewardship campaign, featuring the logo "God Is Able," included a letter each week from the pastor to all member households. Tithing was encouraged. The October 26 letter said, "If you are not presently a tither, let God begin teaching you the blessedness of tithing this Friday or Sunday." A catered stewardship banquet held the first Saturday evening in November drew 90 church members. In the November 3 letter the pastor mentioned the faith promise card on which members were asked to make a one-year pledge to both "Operating/Mission Budget" and to "our Building Fund." Members were urged to bring pledge cards to the banquet or to church on Commitment Sunday (November 8). In a final letter (November 20), Pastor Green wrote, "I realize your commitment was not made to me or even to the church but to God. But I can't help feeling a sense of pride and excitement at your exercise of faith and good stewardship."

Like many pastors, Dick Green does not want to know who pledges what amount. Only the financial secretary records the pledges and sends the receipts. Some members feel strongly about secrecy in this regard. Green's feelings are not unusual in this sensitive area:

> While I think giving levels are an indication of people's spiritual life, I don't want unintentionally to treat people differently because of what they do or do not give. I would want to treat each

member with equal value. I would hope that knowing what they give wouldn't influence me, but I don't know that for sure. But I have told our various financial secretaries over the years that if someone suddenly stops who has been a regular giver, I need to know. That may indicate some crisis or problem in their lives—you know, a medical emergency, or they've lost a job. Just so I can do a pastoral check to see if something's gone wrong financially or emotionally. Is some kind of ministry called for?

Actual giving is high at Northkirk. Pledged contributions and loose plate offerings in 1995 totaled slightly over $165,000, or $1,155 per member. Even more remarkable is that this giving level has been sustained in the face of a building fund drive coinciding with purchase of the present church building. A second drive began in May 1996 in conjunction with a denomination-sponsored financial-services agency. As Darel Griffin pointed out, agency staff members usually suggest first contacting potential large donors. That was not done because "we're not a rich church. We don't have the doctors, the lawyers, the professionals. We have a lot of teachers, but we don't have high-salaried people here." He and Dick Green both found it remarkable that the second campaign had already garnered pledges in excess of $225,000 with no diminution of regular giving. Both attributed high giving to high involvement, a relationship borne out by most research on church giving. But Northkirk also enjoyed the assistance of local Presbyterian churches, having helped in the formation of a four-church "cluster" in the area. As Darel Griffin remarked,

> We had a kind of fund-raising thing with those four. They gave us $6,000 at that time to help us purchase this place. Aside from this welcome help, though, all the giving has come directly from a hundred and fifty people or less. And not in a time of economic prosperity in southern California, either. We're in a church that is giving higher each year and continuing to grow. We're a kind of exception. And all this without the help of the larger denomination. Pretty remarkable.

Griffin's wife, Joretta, active as a leader in the parish, added her own reflection:

I certainly don't think Dick emphasizes money at all. If anything, it's an emphasis on belonging, on family, on involvement and giving out compliments on how many are involved in the church. He recognizes Sunday school teachers. He says and does things that make people feel good about being a part of this church. And yet Dick's a very quiet person who has an effect through the pulpit and through programming and making people feel proud to belong here.

It is little wonder that by the end of 1998, church membership had grown from 150 to 170. That the stewardship approach to money at Northkirk appears to be working is evident from the comment of a church member that appeared in *The Northkirk News*. Firm expectations are perhaps the key:

I feel positive about our program because it starts with the assumption that every member already plans to give financial support for our church. To me, it feels better to be respected and led than it does to be punished.

## Stewardship of Prayer

Prayer enjoys a salient emphasis at Northkirk. As an example, "Telecare" is listed among congregational support ministries: Volunteers contact members and nonmembers on a regular basis for prayer requests, needs, and referrals. Worship lay leaders assist Dick Green at services and represent Northkirk at combined services with other congregations, leading Scripture reading, prayer, and responsive readings. "Prayer-chain" leader and participants agree to pray on a regular basis for needs expressed by the congregation. "Prayer partners" support pastor and congregation during church services and on specific days during the month. I asked Darel Griffin if the emphasis on prayer was something new at Northkirk.

No, it really goes way back. We do several different things. More recently we have what we call a "service of wholeness," a time set aside on Sunday evening once every two months. People can come and share their prayer concerns and be prayed for by one of the pastors and a layperson and experience the laying on of hands. Although it is not a highly attended service, it's a very committed one in terms of prayer. But different people come and go, so it's not the same group time in and time out.

Joretta Griffin expanded:

Some of us feel free to invite people from other churches or communities. As we see them and know their needs, we'll say, "Why don't you come over Sunday night and let us pray for you?" It's done in a quiet and dignified, loving way. Nothing sensational. Just a quiet time of sincere prayer for one another.

Prayer extends to the environment of small-group ministries at Northkirk. As Dick Green pointed out, in addition to the prayer and mutual support they provide, groups are also encouraged to have some kind of mission. "We have a women's group that meets weekly for prayer-and-share. They're studying the Gospel of John right now, but also are involved in the project I mentioned for unwed mothers." The women's group also went on a retreat earlier in the year. Darel Griffin has organized a men's group and was planning a group retreat when I spoke with him.

## Reflection: Great Expectations

The vitality and spirituality evident in this small suburban church might well be accounted for, at first glance, by its small size. One could easily say that a "family spirit" is not hard to generate with fewer than 200 members. But Northkirk goes far beyond this conventional wisdom. With its emphases on spiritual-gift discernment, prayer, and spiritual-growth opportunities for both men and women, this congregation provides a powerful motivational dynamic for engagement in ministry and for generous giving to both church and missions. Is it any wonder that its per-capita revenues, capital-drive contributions (e.g., the loan program), and mission giving are on the high end for any Presbyterian church—and this with a working class/white-collar congregation of modest incomes?

In addition, Northkirk takes on the characteristic of "strict churches" with its message to new-member classes that unless they are prepared to be active in both ministry and financial support, "We still love you, but you may not be ready." In the vocabulary of church growth, it "costs" to belong to Northkirk. Add to this the empowerment encouraged by a pastor who feels comfortable delegating and ceding a good deal of control to his staff and to church members as they undertake responsibilities in ministry (while he himself takes on the challenge of teaching the junior-high group). "Why not?" rather than "Well, let's go slow here" seems to characterize Northkirk's overall climate. In other words, stewardship thrives in this milieu of high expectation and high participation, imaginative programming, and generous willingness to support the congregation, its pastor, and its missions. The congregation is also, of course, blessed by an unusually experienced and gifted associate pastor and his wife. A truly remarkable statistic is that, by 1998, average attendance at Sunday worship services was around 160, very close to the reported size of the congregation!

High expectation and participation are also a product of Dick Green's carefully crafted stewardship sermons, such as the one outlined in this chapter. Sacrificial giving is never an easy message to preach, but Green is forthright in basing his message on New Testament texts (the widow's mite) and, impressively for me, in his invocation of the Christian community in the Acts of the Apostles as a model for Northkirk's giving. After all, Northkirk's small size is a reflection of these early communities, and Green knows how to build on this association. Generous giving results in the community's own needs being met and in God being glorified, Green points out, citing the impression the early Christians made on their neighbors by generously giving to one another. The pastor is also quick to acknowledge the parish's generosity and to tell of his "pride and excitement in their exercise of faith and good stewardship." Nor can one ignore Green's own example in volunteering to teach the church's young people, an example of servant leadership in action.

A key question posed by some church members is whether Northkirk can continue to maintain its dynamism if and when it grows past its present "family size." The question takes on urgency because of the church's location in southern California's "Inland Empire," San Bernardino and Riverside counties. In 1998 the area was one of the fastest-growing in California. Although it will literally take a new millennium to give us the answer, my own guess is that Northkirk's stewardship-driven spirituality, concern with mission outreach, and formation of its young people can flourish as the congregation grows, particularly if the growth is gradual, as now seems to be the case. These features are exactly what many families and individuals are seeking in a church today.

## CHAPTER 9

# OUR NIGHT SHELTER GIVES HELP TONIGHT, HOPE TOMORROW

*First Presbyterian Church, Fort Worth, Texas*

This big downtown church of slightly over 2,000 members, with an average Sunday attendance of 625, celebrated its 125th anniversary in 1998. First Presbyterian Church in Fort Worth, Texas, offers a first-rate example of "institutional stewardship." Having more than its share of prominent and well-off citizens who take pride in Fort Worth's cultural traditions (one thinks of the yearly Van Cliburn piano competition), this church has succeeded in inspiring members to respond to civic needs that arise in this city of 495,000 (metropolitan area of 1,570,000). Outstanding pastoral leadership has played a major role. The Rev. Dr. Robert Bohl was senior pastor from 1980 until 1996. Noted nationally as an outstanding preacher and administrator, he was elected moderator of the 206th General Assembly of the Presbyterian Church (U.S.A.) for 1994-1995. In 1996 he accepted a call as pastor of Village Presbyterian Church in Prairie Village, Kansas, one of the largest Presbyterian churches in the United States. My visit in September 1996 occurred during the search for his replacement. The Rev. Todd Freeman, youth minister, gave me a helpful interview, and in 1998, the new senior pastor, the Rev. Dana Jones, kindly forwarded an informational packet updating the activities and ministries of the church. A subsequent phone conversation with former pastor Bohl provided additional valuable information and insights.

A first brief glimpse of stewardship at First Presbyterian came from Todd Freeman:

This church is certainly blessed with members who have resources, but stewardship here has never been mainly financial. It's always been just as much about volunteer time and talents with which you are blessed. We provide volunteer cards. People go through a list of things they can volunteer for.

A good deal more revealing was an entire taped sermon on stewardship, "First Fruits," mailed by Dana Jones, addressing the topic in his inaugural "stewardship season" in fall 1998. I quote from it at length because I consider it among the most eloquent examples of how an experienced pastor can preach on the stewardship of money and wealth while refusing to identify stewardship with fund-raising. Quite the contrary: Stewardship is indeed an invitation (that may be turned down) beckoning parishioners to awareness of mission. Obstacles to this ideal are formidable.

> We need to resist "the big church," "status quo," "stable," "we've made it," "maintenance now," the temptation to stockpile, to grow reserves for their own sake, safety for its own sake, security for its own sake, sound fiscal policy for its own sake. Rather, salt that has not lost its taste, emptying every day, coming back in, filling up, out again. It is shameful that over and against the pain of the children of this world, the church catholic is often a wealthy stockpiler of goods and things and money for its own sake. We should be mindful of reserves, mindful of security and sound policy and responsible investment in and for the future—I know that. But a church is not a bank. And churches that are just sitting out there, sitting on it, need to start handing out cups of milk, buying lumber, righting wrong, sending forth, so what's left in the books is more like sandals and staff than piles of gold and silver. There are churches preoccupied, almost obsessed, with money. It becomes an idol; it dominates their corporate life; they gather and count and recount and plan and protect and fight and draft policies and, most of all, they just love their money. Get a life! God save us from such idolatry, wastefulness, and self-indulgence here. . . . Stewardship must be fresh and surprising and exciting, because it is in response to God's call, and that is new every morning; in response to God's love, and that is new every morning.

Pastor Jones continued by reminding the congregation of the "ten trillion dollars changing hands in the next 20 years; an unprecedented shift in resources of staggering potential." For First Presbyterian, that could mean a "breakthrough," even "extravagant, creative giving." A new vision is needed, he suggested: New projects include evangelism, justice, and "deepening." New buildings needed will be a legacy "to hand over to our children . . . we need to get young and crowded in here." The church is called to be "a sending place for missionaries near and far."

We need to continue to love and lead and "lean into" this good city. We need to speak truth to power in the public square, join in the hard work of communities and neighborhoods and parenting. We need to faithfully be a strong anchoring place for the larger Presbyterian family of which we are a part, generously enabling mission and ministry. . . . Do more than you can or should. It is not about money or how much money; it is in the laughter! Before you give, listen! And wonder! And laugh! Somewhere from in there, give. . . .

We'll plan to do what we can here within decent and orderly Presbyterian boundaries. But we will be happier and probably most faithful when we ignore those boundaries.

Now you have been magnificent in the wilderness and since. But it's never, ever enough. We are not settling in, we are not settling down here; we are just getting started again. Equipped not for institutional success and well-being; equipped for mission! Estimates vary, but hundreds of thousands of North Korean, Balkan, African children are sick and dying in these weeks because they are hungry while church stewardship campaigns debate reserves, count and recount. Feed the kids, for God's sake! How much to give next year? How much is enough? Laugh and cry and shake your head and say it's impossible; in awesome wonder, helplessly, give your heart! It's about crossing the street with books and bandages and food and medicine and houses and good news, saws and hammers and cribs and hope time after time. . . .

I don't have any interest, finally, in keynoting this stewardship season with numbers or strategies or dollar goals. It isn't about money. I am really very serious about that. I want to say it in the most pastoral tone: If it's about money for you, keep it! Until it's about something else for you, no one needs to give or spend any money to be here, to do anything here if you don't want to give. Don't! The provision we exhaust week after week is God! And of all the things I worry about in my day, the least is that God's provision will ever be insufficient for what God will have us do here. Stir willing hearts–or not? More to do; more to care for . . . It's, do we want to? Tell me about our hearts; "realistic data" are not boundaries for the God of burning bushes, parted waters, and empty tombs. Is it God's work, God's purpose, God's mission? Then here, tell me what amount is all we can do? . . . Stewardship at First Presbyterian Church, on the table, for the first time between us–no flash, no sophisticated programs, no paid consultants, no visits, no pressure–a few comments for a few Sundays, a couple of letters, some information, and we're done. Either we're in a relationship here with God steadily that calls forth first fruits; or, if not stirred and willing, then we can just graze, we can do holiday baskets, we can protect our money. But again, if you feel the wind blowing in this house day after day like I do, if you hear *your name*–imagine, your name!–blowing in that wind, if your heart knows an excitement, a touch so extraordinary it could burst; if in this place you are compelled to risk, to be foolish, to hope and dream in ways that surprise who you really are out there; if you do anything you could for a lost child; if Jesus is Lord for you, then let's get on with it. But if someone is still grumbling–you know, saying maybe it's not fair, I do enough–tell me, as we gather at the foot of the Cross, tell me about "fair."

Let me be unmistakably "fair": for those who hate stewardship appeals, who wish they hadn't come this morning, wish they'd known ahead of time what I was going to preach on, don't like churches asking for money, especially for more money, for those who are convinced they just do enough–they send in the same number every year no matter what–well, here's the best news, the fairest news: keep it; keep all of it. Don't worry about it! Just come here and be with us. It's all free for you. If you don't want to do more, then I don't want you to . . . don't give a thing next year. You have this minister's OK in our first stewardship sermon together. Spend it on something more important. Or just treasure it. But the good news, as we say here–on the other hand, always over and against–the good news is, you can give much more if you want to. Next year, I rise this morning to report, there will be more to do, much more. We'll need more to do it with, much more. In this, I need your hearts. That's always been enough here, and it always will be. The Spirit has made us restless together. God will provide. Amen.

Pastor Jones is aware, as is any pastor of a big, historic, and still active downtown church, of the size of the 1999 budget with its multiple forms of outreach and service. These "basics" form the background to his eloquence. A long list of "specific benevolences" totals $1,281,500. Generous support for synod and presbytery alone comes to $412,500, the largest single entry. Next is "undesignated mission funds," coming to $400,000. The Presbyterian Night Shelter (see below) takes up another $110,000 and reflects the local character of the remaining benevolences: Fort Worth is the chief beneficiary, as it has been for over a century, of this "big church" literally in its midst.

Budgeted cash disbursements come to $3,098,200 and cover territory familiar to Presbyterians: evangelism, Presbyterian Women, congregational care, long-range planning, stewardship, administrative costs, staff, etc. The single largest entry is $1,281,500 for missions (doubtless including the hungry youngsters overseas Pastor Jones singled out). Endowments form a healthy source of cash, as well. Over $700,000 comes from investments of various kinds, smaller amounts from designated contributions and "all other."

As in most Presbyterian churches, pledging is counted on to raise the balance needed–$2,125,200–after cash receipts. The total number of potential pledging units is slightly over 1,000; Pastor Jones reported that 1999 actual pledges totaled approximately 700. While the actual overall amount pledged is not available at this writing, if the balance needed is met, each pledging unit will give approximately from $2,200 to $3,000–impressive numbers indeed.

Ways of encouraging pledging have varied, as Todd Freeman explained:

We've gone all the way from a "Pony Express," where a pledge packet is taken from one home to another in succession, to having some of our elders volunteer to do house visits. I don't think you can ever do one program more than a couple of years in a row. In Dr. Bohl's absence, we had four speakers on stewardship last Sunday. One spoke on world missions, another [speaking] on local missions [is a member] whose mother is over at the Alzheimer's clinic; then the stewardship chair spoke on . . . this year's campaign, and finally myself on youth ministry. Someone spoke of our youth as "the future of the church," which I hate! They are also the "now" of the church. You don't just wait until they're older before you consider them fully as people!

Patrick Reardon, 1996 stewardship committee chair, told me that door-to-door soliciting for pledges "does not work in a Presbyterian community. People aren't used to being asked in person to pledge, and they don't like it." Asking for pledges in church during stewardship campaigns is the way to proceed, he thought, giving members full information about the ministries the church is supporting.

For every dollar taken in, First Presbyterian gives half to missions, a practice continued in the 1999 budget (funds labeled "mission" totaling over $1.6 million out of an overall budget of approximately $3 million-and this excludes gifts to specific local benevolences). It also (in both 1996 and 1999) had been supporting 25 percent of the entire budget for the presbytery, a yearly sum of about $400,000. Freeman remarked that although the church is the third largest in Grace Presbytery, it is the highest giver. Under Pastor Jones, along with the One Great Hour of Sharing collection taken in the spring that goes to the national church, First Presbyterian also participates in the Peacemaking and Christmas offerings of the denomination, puts on numerous fund-raisers, and takes special offerings at Sunday morning worship services.

## Institutional Stewardship

A paragraph from First Presbyterian's mission statement forms a fitting introduction to the idea of institutional stewardship:

> We acknowledge our obligation to be Christ's servants in the world, and we work to meet that responsibility through missions of service and ministries of compassion.

One basic ingredient for this form of stewardship is firmly in place at First Presbyterian: a sizable cadre of prominent as well as financially successful and well-connected members who respond to respected pastoral leadership.

Pastor Robert Bohl's approach was to engage in direct, one-on-one pastoral contact with older and more affluent church members, working with them to set up financial instruments such as charitable gift annuities. In the latter, donor and church become partners, the donor receiving income until his or her decease, when the church benefits directly from the annuity. Sizable gifts were also given outright to First Presbyterian when he was pastor of the church, and form the basis of the church's large endowment.

Three expressions of institutional stewardship stand out:

1. *Presbyterian Night Shelter of Tarrant County.* The terrible winter of 1983-1984 in Fort Worth brought about a crisis: Shelters providing services to homeless people were overflowing. A homeless man crawled into an abandoned van to protect himself from below-zero weather and froze to death. Responding to this tragic news, the Rev. J. W. Jablonowski, Jr., pastor of St. Stephen's Presbyterian Church, met with Pastor Bohl. They determined that the need for a free shelter in Tarrant County was too great to ignore any longer. Together with the pastor of Ridglea Presbyterian Church, they called on community leaders to help in the formation of a nonprofit corporation to start a night shelter for homeless people. Foundations as well as a broader spectrum of churches were enlisted to support the new venture. Beginning in a school building in December 1984, the shelter drew increasing numbers of homeless people until, by 1987, demand for services occasioned the opening of a new center. Open 24 hours a day, seven days a week, Presbyterian Night Shelter (PNS) provides, in the words of its general information flyer:

> For anyone who is homeless, a clean, safe place to sleep, showers and toilet facilities, a hot meal every evening, sandwiches and coffee for breakfast, and coats and blankets. It is free to anyone for as long as needed between the hours of 5 P.M. and 5 A.M. Families with children under 17 and those with medical problems may stay for free around the clock.

A dispensary staffed by volunteers from First Presbyterian and elsewhere distributes toiletries, hygiene items, and over-the-counter medicines on a daily basis. A small playroom features books and toys available to children. Again, volunteers "donate time and love to our kids, to read with them, and to lead structured activities."

The shelter employs 25 homeless individuals, "who are paid competitive wages for work that is performed." A full-time social worker helps with a variety of services, including assistance in job-seeking, applying for AFDC (Aid to Families with Dependent Children) and food stamps, and applying for housing. A "PNS Network" enlists the cooperation of such agencies as the Department of Veterans Affairs, the Tarrant County Mental Health and Mental Retardation Center, and the John Peter Smith Health Clinic. These agencies provide a range of services to help participants "regain emotional stability and/or sobriety, reacquire job-readiness skills, obtain housing, and to eventually achieve self-sufficiency." The health clinic uses the services of volunteer physicians. A representative of the Fort Worth community on the board of directors oversees administration of the shelter. First Presbyterian's Night Shelter Auxiliary helps to coordinate fund-raising and volunteer efforts. With justifiable pride, a recent shelter newsletter relates, "[T]o date, PNS has provided over 1,328,000 nights of stay and served more than 2.5 million meals to homeless citizens, and remains the only 'free' homeless shelter."

Concern for the homeless continues. Current (1999) projects of First Presbyterian are the construction of a separate women's and children's building for the homeless, together with a "Safe Haven." Designed for the homeless who are mentally ill, the Safe Haven will be jointly funded by a number of public agencies–federal, county, and local–as well as by private foundations and public donations. A recent appeal for support illustrates the compassion that informs the entire homeless ministry and marks it as a church-sponsored outreach mission:

> Safe Havens came about because the government realized that upon closure of many mental institutions, many of the people who had lived in them for years had no other place to go except the streets. These are the people that you see in downtown areas, wearing ragged clothing, doing strange or unnatural things, talking to someone or something that no one except that person can see. You know, the ones we don't like to look at. The ones we like to pretend aren't there. But they are. . . . We have needed a place where people who are so ill that they cannot live in shelters, yet not ill enough to be forcibly placed in a hospital, can go, other than jail. . . . The Safe Haven will provide that safe, warm place . . . [and] will be staffed with trained individuals who will

work to become attuned to the residents' needs, gain their trust, and help them lead as productive a life as they are able to.

2. *The James L. West Presbyterian Special Care Center.* James West was a leading citizen in Fort Worth's business, religious, and civic life, and an active member of First Presbyterian Church. When Alzheimer's disease claimed his life, the James L. and Eunice West Charitable Trust made a gift through First Presbyterian to provide major funding, through a nonprofit corporation, for construction of a nondenominational facility, the first of its kind in the state of Texas. When it opened in the summer of 1993, it was described as "dedicated to providing a loving environment for persons with Alzheimer's disease and related disorders and compassionate support for their families."

The center's medical staff, supervised by a physician director, includes registered nurses, licensed vocational nurses, certified nursing assistants, and a pharmacist. Support staff consists of social workers, activity therapists, and dieticians. Trained volunteers round out the West Center's team, "which is dedicated to creating an environment that reflects the most modern, compassionate, and effective care." The same spirit of compassion animating the night shelter is at work in the center. Continuing from the center's information flyers,

> The West Center's professionals understand the impact of Alzheimer's disease and related disorders upon other family members. Family visits are encouraged and the family is informed and included in the resident's ongoing treatment program. In addition, knowledgeable professionals work to meet the specific needs of the family/caregivers by offering support, counseling, and access to community resources.

This four-story facility also offers a "Senior Adult Day Care Program." Caregivers can bring a patient to the center for a half day or full day. Available services for day-care patients embrace health monitoring, medications, two meals per day, individualized activities (recreation, music, and exercise therapy), social-worker services, religious services, dietary consultation, and transportation for group outings. The fourth floor is designed for patients "whose physical condition requires additional nursing care. A hospice-like environment is provided in the final stage of illness to

ensure the highest possible degree of comfort and dignity for residents."
Medicare and private insurance cover most costs for resident patients, but
as a nonprofit corporation, the center specifies that "we strive to admit
without regard to ability to pay." Financial assistance is available to those
needing it.

Once again, the tone of the center's literature suggests a religiously
inspired institution in which caring and compassion are readily discern-
ible and available.

3. *Habitat for Humanity*. The Fort Worth Area Habitat for Humanity
counts First Presbyterian as one of its supporting institutions. Corporations
and businesses contribute in diverse ways to Habitat by lending financial
support, at times labor as well as building materials. But as the local (Fort
Worth) Habitat "History and Mission" statement indicates, "The majority
of the support for new buildings still comes from local faith groups and
mission organizations." Faith Presbyterian "has contributed in excess of
$100,000 each year for the past two years [1997 and 1998] and has com-
mitted the same for 1999." As 1997 ended, Fort Worth Habitat had completed 52 homes in the city. By the beginning of 1999, 17 of these had
been built by First Presbyterian, through both volunteer assistance and
mission dollars.

## Volunteering Time and Talent

As Todd Freeman pointed out, stewardship at First Presbyterian has always emphasized volunteering and active participation in ministries. To
cite one example: In Presbyterian congregations, all women church members are regarded as members of "Presbyterian Women." How active the
organization is varies, of course, from church to church. At First Presbyterian, it is most impressive. As of 1999, almost 400 women were active,
organized into 19 "circles." A fairly elaborate organizational structure
includes the following departments: program, Bible, Christian fellowship,
prayer, and Christian action. Committees within the various departments
reveal the range of activities: Christian growth, ecumenical missions, national missions, special events, projects, layette room, gift workshop, circle
membership, nominating, clothing room, communion, finance, publicity,
flowers, decorations, and ad hoc. Generous support by members enables

"PW" to bring in speakers and workshop moderators of national reputation. Themes and activities have included tolerance and open-mindedness,
a worship "Service of Wholeness," mission speakers, Bible study programs,
and leadership training. Members of other churches are often invited to
attend. Retreats are offered and events scheduled with other PW groups in
Grace Presbytery and the Synod of the Sun. Delegates attend the yearly
Churchwide Gathering of PW.

Fund-raising is a serious PW enterprise, as is provision of clothing,
toys, personal hygiene items, etc., for the night shelter, the West Special
Care Center, the John Peter Smith Hospital, United Way, YWCA, and the
Cancer Society. From PW's clothing room alone, more than 40 nonprofit
agencies and school districts in Tarrant County accessed clothing for 203
men, 177 women, and 631 children (1997 church data). A special project
of this PW organization is a "Jail Cookie Ministry" for which more than
10,000 cookies are baked, wrapped, and stored to await delivery to in-
mates in Tarrant County jails just before Christmas. In 1997, over $30,000
was raised to benefit various mission activities.

Todd Freeman served on the boards of two organizations:

1. *I Have a Dream*, a nationwide program begun by a member of First
Presbyterian. It provides support for children from low-income families
(often those in housing projects) who want to stay in school, linking them
with mentors who meet with the children in First Presbyterian's facilities.

2. *The Tarrant County AIDS Interfaith Network.* In 1996 the church
made a $10,000 gift to help the county AIDS program move to a new
facility.

Senior citizens 55 and older are invited to join "The Beacons of First
Presbyterian Church." Beacons serves the social needs of older adults,
providing a monthly potluck supper and various programs. Besides enter-
tainment events ("Birthday Bash" luncheons and out-of-town trips), service projects include church-camp support, Habitat for Humanity, Meals
on Wheels, the donation of Campbell's soup labels to benefit schools, and
minor repairs and services to church property.

New ministries begun in 1997-1998 include a "Green Group" focusing on environmental concerns, a "Welfare to Work" group interested in
helping people move from welfare rolls to gainful employment, an expanded prison ministry, and a "muffin ministry" in which muffins made by
volunteers in the church's kitchen are brought to people in the congregation out of either "concern" or "celebration."

## Worship, Music, Adult Formation

First Presbyterian is blessed with Robert McDonald, a nationally known organist and choir director formerly of Riverside Church, New York, and Radio City Music Hall. A splendid pipe organ, recently upgraded, adds to the high quality of the church's worship services and music ministry. Several paid soloists contribute to a program that includes an annual music series. The church's sanctuary and organ are used by various groups, including the American Guild of Organists and Grace Presbytery. The church's Chancel Choir and adult handbell choir attract visitors from all over Fort Worth.

Adult education, as current pastor Dana Jones expressed it, is a "growing ministry in our church." Lent 1998 featured an emphasis on "Reformed Spirituality," with a special weekend led by Dr. Howard Rice (professor of ministry and chaplain emeritus of San Francisco Theological Seminary) and a six-week course on the topic. A "Disciples Bible Training" program was instituted. Other examples are a six-week course on General Assembly "Washington Issues" during fall 1998. Four 13-week courses are offered in First Presbyterian's adult church school classes. Course titles for 1998-1999 include "Inner Journey," "Spiritual Disciplines," "Contemplative Writers," and "Writings of the Desert Fathers."

## Ministry of Welcome

Pastor Jones contributed the following account of the current welcoming ministry:

> We have greeters in place each Sunday morning to welcome the congregation members as they come into the church. Each Sunday morning prior to the church school hour there is a welcome reception where people can meet and greet each other. Coffee and doughnuts are provided.
>
> We have begun a monthly event called "Stripling Mixer" (held in our Stripling Dining Room). It is designed for new members and longtime members to meet for approximately an hour and a half just to become better acquainted. A light supper is served. A member of the evangelism committee is also in attendance.

The first Sunday of every month name tags are provided for each person attending the service as another means of becoming better acquainted with other members. The tags are distributed through the church school classes and are available also in other entrance areas of the building. Our congregational care commission reviews attendance records of members via the ritual of friendship pages entered into the computer each Monday morning. If a pattern of attendance is broken, contact is made with that member.

## Reflection: Belying the Downtown Mainline Image

Stewardship at First Presbyterian was shaped in no small degree by the personality of Robert Bohl, pastor from 1980 to 1996. His one-on-one approach to affluent donors involved pastoral concern for them, together with reminders that church and community would benefit enormously from their generous gifts. Bohl's work laid the foundation for the institutional stewardship that has borne such fruit in the city of Fort Worth. First Presbyterian became, for all practical purposes, emblematic of mainline churches that became over many decades pillars of the community.

It is, I think, no exaggeration to suggest that such churches are themselves stewards of their communities. Think of the night-shelter idea. In the minds of the two pastors who began it, the community could no longer tolerate human beings freezing to death because no warm shelter was available. The church became prophet, calling citizens' attention to a dire need that aroused public support from institutions as well as individuals. First Presbyterian's members adopted the night shelter as their particular responsibility. One outcome has been a deepening sensitivity to the situation of the homeless, resulting in the construction of the Safe Haven and the separate shelter for mothers and children. Compassion spreads, involving more people, more agencies, and the Fort Worth community itself tackling a responsibility that was not apparent earlier.

Robert Bohl saw a stewardship challenge in working with church members blessed with this world's wealth. "From those who have, much is expected" seems to have been close to a driving conviction for Bohl. Fearless, direct, and creative in one-on-one encounters, he made himself knowledgeable about the world of financial instruments so that he could demonstrate mutual advantage to donor and to church in setting up annuities and trusts. In undertaking this ministry, Bohl seems to have created a climate out of which grew the family gift that eventuated in the James L. West Presbyterian Special Care Center. It is no surprise, either, that First Presbyterian would become an active sponsor of Habitat for Humanity. Institutional stewardship, far from reflecting faceless buildings, actually created avenues and outlets whereby people could involve themselves in ministries of compassion affecting literally thousands in their community.

In 1999, it seems evident that new senior pastor Dana Jones is no less dedicated in his own way to carrying on and even expanding these rich and fruitful traditions. Common to both pastors is a vision of First Presbyterian's identity and mission that made them unafraid to challenge the congregation to undertake stewardship commitments whose thrust and content are far beyond "mere fund-raising."

Stewardship of gifts and talents is abundantly manifest in the ministries and initiatives reviewed above. Presbyterian Women offers a splendid example of an organization that has continued to enlist the creative energies of women and further their Christian formation for more than 125 years. Senior citizens' needs for community building, caring, and giving are met through Beacons. Recent energies have gone into both adult and youth education as well as a welcoming program that many churches could well emulate. First Presbyterian, we can say, belies the images of old downtown mainline churches simply fading away as their members move elsewhere. Visit the congregation's recently created Web site. You will be invited to click on to "our staff," "our history," "our location, " "our music." Those accepting will recognize the continuing vitality of this venerable church as its members "do covenant to move decisively into the future."

## CHAPTER 10

# LIFTING UP A VISION FOR THE CONGREGATION

*Faith Lutheran Church, Seward, Nebraska*

Sometimes a congregation backs into stewardship. Faith Lutheran Church needed a new multipurpose building at a cost of over $350,000. It seemed to the Rev. Robert Moss "an incredible bite financially" for the 326-member congregation he serves in Seward, Nebraska, a town of 5,700. As a first step, members of the church finance committee visited Lutheran parishes in the vicinity that were engaged in building campaigns. A committee member recalled:

> We found a church in Lincoln that used the Resident Steward-ship Service (RSS) out of our national ELCA [Evangelical Lutheran Church in America] office in Chicago. We contacted RSS. They would help us raise funds only if we did a steward-ship drive at the same time. They wouldn't help us just raise money for a building addition.

An initial hesitancy occurred when a church member who had been a fund-raiser for Big Brothers and Big Sisters in the community volunteered to head the building drive free of charge. After much deliberation, described by Pastor Moss as "one of the major battles" where stewardship was concerned, the committee decided to decline the "free offer" and pay the consulting fee to bring in RSS.[1]

That contact was the key to beginning stewardship at Faith Lutheran. For almost 40 years, RSS has been offering educational and consulting services to Lutheran congregations around the United States. The denomination seems truly blessed in this regard. When Stan Rose, one of RSS's principal consultants, arrived from Chicago, he sat down with pastor and finance committee and launched into a study of the biblical basis for stewardship. In the words of an RSS brochure, "[A]ll members are invited . . .

to explore the meaning of response to the Gospel, and consider personal commitment to the Lord. Increased giving in all dimensions of life, including money, happens when this study takes place."

Given the impetus from Stan Rose and the vision he imparted, Moss quickly saw what the program could bring:

> It wasn't fund-raising per se, but it was overall stewardship. What we wanted was a way we could help our people be enthusiastic in their response to what God had already done for them. Too, we wanted to raise our vision for what our mission could be through our building. While our initial thought was how we could fund a building program, we ended up realizing that we needed to develop beneath that a foundational stewardship program. This had never been done. The roots of our congregation being mostly rural, giving was very seasonal. And pledging was a big no-no, a big taboo.

*You mean no pledging at all?*

> I mean no pledging at all. It was referred to simply as "the P word," and we don't! Part of all this is due to what some of our older parishioners remember, like "When I was a kid in the church and we fell behind in our pledge, they came knocking on the door saying 'you owe us.'" Whether that was actually said or not, that's the way it was heard. So we try not to offend. We may always live with this idea pretty loosely. For right now we don't mess with that.

But with a finance committee that renamed itself the stewardship committee (during a meeting that Moss was unable to attend), Moss saw lay leadership arise to make a big difference:

> The head of that committee, Don, has really been the driving force behind our stewardship program. He has faced the congregational elements and just plowed in and done an outstanding, in fact, incredible job of lifting up a vision for the congregation that people respond to. That vision is really necessary, I've come to understand, because today there are so many ways people

can give. They're going to give where it will do the most good, where the most ministry will be accomplished, whether it be Red Cross, the Heart Association, United Way or whatever. So you have to create a vision that's high enough and big enough that's worthy of their time. Worthy to consider writing a check for. For us that springboard was the building. Everyone recognized the inadequacy of our facility. That was something we could raise up quite easily and build a stewardship program underneath.

As Moss and the stewardship council discovered, though, pledging for a building addition was one matter, but pledging for general giving quite another. The emphasis when I visited was on "first fruits," in which the initial check one writes after getting paid is to a charitable cause, preferably to the church. Stewardship at Faith Lutheran, then, began within a broad frame–a giving according to the donor's sense of priority within the context of "first fruits."

Moss also believes that financial stewardship enables congregation members to feel more a part of their community. The various programs and activities, "whether it be the WIC [Women, Infants, and Children program] clinic that uses our facility, or the immunization clinic, or an AA [Alcoholics Anonymous] group, or Sunday School, or even candles on the altar at worship–you feel you're brought in to be a part of all that. I think it needs to be articulated along with things that happen outside the facility as well." Like a lot of pastors, Moss wants his congregation to know where "the 20 percent of our budget that we give away" goes. Bringing in representatives of various groups and activities the church sponsors is vital–"to come in and say exactly what it is that you as members of a congregation are part of. Here's what you are supporting." As an example, he cited students from the University of Nebraska Lutheran Student Center, on whose board he serves. Simply appearing at his church to share with the congregation their ministry to fellow students is a big step toward encouraging willingness to give.

In other words, if members concretely see causes worthy of writing a check for, they will support that effort rather than something else like United Way. This is a critical stewardship challenge, as the pastor sees it. More pointedly, he is convinced that the stewardship committee plays a vital role in easing church members' reluctance to discuss money in the first place:

As soon as you start talking money, you just see the walls go up: "Don't you talk to me about that." People would rather talk about sex, they'd rather talk about religion, they'd rather talk about politics—about any personal issue rather than money. Part of the duty of a stewardship committee is to break that down and tell people, reveal to people, and live out for people, that it really is OK to talk about money because that, too, is a gift from God. And therefore it's part of your response: how you serve, how you respond to living out your faith in God who is active in your life. It's difficult, though. At Faith here, a significant number of people are still not going to tell you what they give. "I'll just give, but I'm not going to tell you how much I'm going to give. That is none of your business." As I've said before, pledging for these people is simply a no-no.

## A 1998 Update

Stewardship of money, by the end of 1998, had taken firm root. Overall giving in 1996 totaled $179,149, but that included funds given for the building drive, as well as a special "decorating fund" for painting, wallpaper, and new carpet in the older building. Many of these donations were given as a one-time "Give a Christmas Gift to the Church" in December 1996. It was no surprise, then, that the 1997 total dropped to $156,077. In 1998, however, overall giving rose to $170,501, a 9.25 percent increase over the previous year, due in no small part to a single gift of $20,000 from one family. At first glance, considering that total membership had changed very little since 1996—327 individuals, 135 households, average Sunday attendance around 130—Faith Lutheran was doing very well among Lutheran congregations nationwide. Per-member giving in 1993, according to national data I helped to collect, was $415; per-household giving came to $746. The respective figures for Faith Lutheran are $525 and $1,322. Pledging members, however, are the key to this high giving. Between 1996 and 1998, the stewardship committee had invited members to pledge to both the general fund and a building fund. Only 30 adult households pledged in 1997 and 1998, but their general fund pledges—$55,597 in 1997 and $51,817 in 1998—accounted for 61 percent of the 1997 general fund total of $90,578, and 55 percent of the 1998 total of $93,703.

Pledgers' building fund contributions came to about a third of the total contributed in both years. Overall, the average 1998 pledge was an impressive $1,720.

Another factor: By 1997, Faith Lutheran was utilizing national ELCA's "Growth Giving Challenge." The worksheet provided asks Lutheran church members "to increase your giving through the congregation by one percent of your weekly income, and to consider similar growth at least annually, moving toward and beyond a tithe (10%)." Below this explanation is a chart (now quite widely used in several denominations) listing weekly income in one column and weekly giving percentages in succeeding columns. The range is from one percent through 15 percent. A similar worksheet is provided for children, substituting "weekly allowance or income" for "weekly income." A kind of "mirror effect" enables members to see what they give in terms of specific percentages; e.g., if I am made aware that my giving comes to only one percent of my income, I may take stock and become more intentional about what I (we) decide to give.

Clearly, however, the challenge to Faith Lutheran, and to any congregation, is to increase the number of those making pledges. The challenge is especially acute in denominations like the ELCA, in which pledging is not as traditional as it is among Presbyterians. But to leave it at that would be seriously misleading. By 1998, Faith Lutheran's council and congregation committed themselves "to giving the first 16% of general fund gifts to meet our mission share (benevolence) commitments, which help the needs of the ELCA throughout the state, country, and world" (1998 stewardship committee report). More than $21,000, over and above general-fund and building-fund offerings, was given to a variety of missions, including World Hunger, ELCA Global Mission, and others. The entire church Christmas offering went to Nebraska Lutheran Outdoor Ministries and to Lutheran Family Services. Lenten supper donations went toward medical bills for a seriously ill church member.

Closely related is the congregation's Board of Mission Outreach. "Social ministry" includes members of a "prayer chain," who offer prayers for three days in response to requests "for people or special causes." Also supported are donations to a food pantry, gifts for a selected "Christmas family," and quilts, made by "WELCA [Women of the ELCA] Quilters," distributed to needy families in the county. An evangelism group makes personal visits to families and individuals who have visited the church during the year and marked "interested" on attendance sheets available in the pews.

As a next step, the stewardship committee in fall 1998 invited a representative of Planned Giving Services for the ELCA's Nebraska Synod to hold a workshop on wills, estates, and gift planning. At year's end, an endowment fund had been set up with an initial investment of $925.

## Enlisting Time and Talents

Rob Moss reflected on a theology of service that underlies this dimension of stewardship at Faith Lutheran:

> I think that, as Christian people, now that we've been saved by God's grace, God has done everything on our behalf, has died and ensured our life. Now that's salvation, but where does discipleship come in? As Christian people we've been called by God into this body, the church, to do something. The church does not exist so we can get into heaven. I don't believe that. It exists as an institution so that we can serve. And we are the ones called by God into that church to serve. I honestly believe we'll get a better response from people in the long run if we emphasize and kind of pick at their need to give, not just get something back. I just don't think that's good motivation; instead it's selfish.

Pastor and stewardship committee developed together a 16-page sign-up brochure that could serve as a model for any local church. The first option is to volunteer for the monthly "Saints in Service." Twelve teams, one for each month, are organized by two families serving as team leaders. A parishioner can check one or more of the following roles: greeter, usher, lesson reader, acolyte, communion assistant, altar guild, coffee host, cleaning committee, and team leader. Subsequent pages are each prefaced by "Making Christ Known." No activity is merely assumed or taken for granted. Thus, one can, under "Individual Participation," check off worshipping regularly; attending Sunday school/adult Sunday school; having daily devotions; communing regularly; praying for the congregation, congregational members, and pastor; and making a financial commitment to Christ's mission through faith. Elected congregational positions form the next list, from president through "Gifts of Faith" endowment committee. Serving on the board of trustees involves "being responsible for the care and upkeep of the material properties of the congregation." Working on grounds and landscaping, on buildings, doing painting, electrical work, plumbing, mowing, and snow removal are some of the check-off possibilities.

The page labeled "Social Ministry" calls for a two-year commitment of once-a-month meetings. Sign-up possibilities include providing monetary support for "our missionaries in Cameroon" (they are named), helping with the social ministry of the board of mission outreach cited above, working on ecumenical programs, participating in the September CROP Walk, and not insignificantly, "discovering [community needs and encouraging] action to meet those needs." Another page extends this kind of volunteering to community activities and organizations such as a community blood bank, a hospital auxiliary, various civic clubs (e.g., Rotary and Kiwanis), Parent-Teacher Association, and senior citizen (or youth) committees in Seward.

The front cover aptly sets forth the parish mission statement that undergirds all activities and imparts a sense of purpose:

> Faith Lutheran Church, a community of believers, seeks to proclaim the Gospel of Jesus Christ to all people. We seek to provide a welcoming and caring environment where all people can experience the help, hope and love of Jesus Christ.

The concluding page asks church members to state which areas of ministry "could be enhanced . . . could be implemented . . . could be reevaluated."

Following the advice of Stan Rose, the RSS consultant, the parish's drive to sign up volunteers for ministries was undertaken at a different time of year from stewardship devoted to fund-raising. Don Rondorf, currently president of the congregation, links the generous turnout of volunteers partly to development of the mission statement. "If people understand what the vision of this congregation is—and there was no such thing when my wife and I started here—you won't have any problem getting volunteers for ministries." Rondorf also believes that "it's easier straight off" to get people to volunteer their time than to get them to give money. Work on enhancing volunteering first, he suggests. This opens the door to increased giving, but if a church emphasizes financial giving first, it's by no means certain that volunteering will follow.

Rondorf reflected on the urgency of getting new members on board as soon as possible.

> The part we sometimes miss, and [we've] still [got to] work on it here, is when you get somebody coming in new, get them involved right away. If we don't get them involved when they come right down the chute, if you miss them the first two or three weeks or a month, you never get them involved. But once they get going, they tend to see the involvement as growth within themselves as well as for the church and for the community.

Humor comes into play during new-member classes. Members of parish boards and committees put on a skit. Pastor Moss elaborates:

> The poor new member coming in is given a shovel or a lawn mower by one of the trustees. A stewardship person gives them a box of envelopes and a threatening note about how much you have to give. The parish education people dump a load of Sunday School material on them and tell them what class they'll be teaching.
>
> Now we do all this for two reasons: one, just to be funny and to share with them some of the opportunities that are there; secondly, to remind ourselves what we need to be doing is inviting people, not pressuring them. Share the opportunities that are available. We know some would jump right in anyway, but others don't. They're not comfortable doing that. Stewardship in this sense is a process. You begin with where people are. If they want to start just with Sunday worship, that's fine. We just keep lifting up opportunities for them and articulating, hopefully, where certain gifts they may have would fit in.

*A lot of people are under time and activity crunches these days. Volunteering costs them.*

> That's absolutely true. Take the nine years I've been here. We used to say, "work day Saturday. We're going to clean inside, outside, shape things up; come on out, everybody." And we'd have tons of people. But over the years that has certainly come

down to a very, very small handful. The thing is, there are so many other programs that people, especially parents, see as worth their time. Kids' soccer, for example. So if I have a choice, as a parent, between something my kid's involved in and raking the church yard, I know where I'm going to be.

Moss has had to acknowledge, as have pastors all over the United States, that "people may not be doing church things." Instead, they may be serving on the PTA, doing something with the Optimist Club, or promoting construction of a youth center downtown. "Is that less valuable ministry?" he asks.

So what we have to do, as a congregation, has got to be valuable ministry as well. We've got to make sure that what we do, we do very well and that it is worthwhile. It has to be significant, relevant ministry or it just won't go. It will fail.

## Reflection: A Shift in Stewardship Attitudes

The stewardship program at Faith Lutheran got off the ground because pastor and congregation decided they needed a solid fund drive to put up a new building. Calling in the Resident Stewardship Service provided by the denomination's national office was decisive in getting the finance (now stewardship) committee to start thinking of stewardship biblically and theologically–a vision shared and fully supported by the pastor. This vision helped pastor and committee members approach every household in the church and ask each to pledge for the building drive.

Getting families and households to pledge was not easy. Many among the older members raised on farms resisted pledging. Farming was (is) a precarious occupation in that farmers don't know whether their crops will come in or what price they will bring. Pledging, then, seems hazardous and is consequently resisted. Younger nonfarm families in the parish often came from churches in which pledging was normative. The challenge for pastor and stewardship committee was to extend the original pledging for the building drive into regular weekly offerings. When I visited the parish in late summer 1996, even though 50 percent of households were on record as pledging, regular offerings were staying the same as before, perhaps understandably, because so many families had extended themselves financially to pledge for the building drive. Pledging was easier to "sell" because of the widespread conviction that the building was truly necessary for the parish. As we have seen, however, solid progress was made over the next two years in overall giving. Pledging was still the province of a small core of households, but a tradition had begun of solid support for general fund, building fund, and mission giving. Faith Lutheran seems to have hit a "take-off" stage in financial stewardship, aided by a dynamic and creative stewardship committee.

Stewardship education through RSS had contributed to a keen sense that members need to be motivated to get involved in church ministries. Strategies for inviting members, new and old, to sign up for ministries seem to have been successful. A useful tool in this respect is a "Time and Talent Booklet" in which members can choose and sign up for ministries. Like many other churches, Faith Lutheran had customarily distributed these booklets in January, marking time and talent as a spring event distinct from the fall stewardship campaign for money. In 1998, the stewardship committee recommended that both be done in the fall to stress the linkage of time, talent, and treasure.

Stewardship, as the pastor pointed out, needed to shift from supporting the building drive (as it had indeed done) to supporting growing ministries mainly through pledged regular offerings. Yet, as Pastor Moss pointed out, a signal benefit of having the Resident Stewardship Service visit the church was its emphasis on the spiritual meaning of stewardship rather than its being identified as a fund-raising activity. It was precisely this emphasis, he believes, that motivated many parishioners to return a larger share of their finances and to enhance participation in ministries. No small part of this enhancement was to make ministries attractive in the face of the many opportunities for service elsewhere in the community, combined with the demands on parents' time as they involve their children in programs whose number and attractiveness have also increased dramatically. "Soccer moms" may have become a cliché, but they serve as a pretty apt symbol for this new competitive milieu in which churches find themselves.

Readers should note, I think, that the successful stewardship initiatives described above were, by 1998-1999, undergirded by an interactive system of committees, with stewardship working closely with the finance and budget committee and both in consultation with the council, the church's governing body. In fact, the vice-president of the council is the chair of the finance and budget committee. This interaction, however, does not obscure the principal mandate of the stewardship committee, which is educational. Its chair, Pam Rondorf, told me that members keep alive the meaning and salience of stewardship by planning each fall's campaign with a distinctive theme ("Noah's Ark and God's Promises to Us" and "The Health of the Body" being two recent examples). In any case, Faith Lutheran provides one more example of the wisdom of maintaining distinctive committees for finance/budget and for stewardship, while ensuring active interchange among all committees charged with planning and supporting the church's overall mission.

At first glance, the experience of Faith Lutheran seems to suggest that embarking on a stewardship emphasis without a tangible objective like putting up a new building may not garner much congregational support. Pastor Moss demurs: "While a physical vision may be easier to articulate, it is not necessarily more effective." Recall his belief that the building campaign was a springboard for articulating "a vision that's high enough and big enough to be worthy of their time" and worth writing a check for. In other words, stewardship, preached insistently with all its theological and biblical roots, *can* provide the concrete motivational dynamic to increase giving levels. A visible target like a building campaign *may* help to get things started, but the pastor does not see a campaign as a *necessary* condition. Articulating a vision is necessary, along with the dynamism of a stewardship committee entrusted with wide responsibilities. This small town/rural church has gone a long way toward "lifting" that vision, evidenced by increased budgets and mission and ministry support as it approaches a new millennium.

## CHAPTER 11

# LIKE A GOLF SWING: AS WE LOSE OURSELVES, WE CONNECT

*Desert Cross Lutheran Church, Tempe, Arizona*

Can a pastor who's an ardent golfer possibly be a respected steward of his parish? The answer is yes, but we'll get to that later. Desert Cross Lutheran Church is the Rev. Steven Holm's third church. He arrived in 1990 after serving a 1,000-member church in Wyoming, whose annual budget hovered around $300,000. He's now in Tempe, a fast-growing neighbor city of Phoenix known mainly as the site of Arizona State University. His congregation numbered 900 members by mid-1998, averaging over 500 at worship on weekends. Total 1997 pledges, plus both plate and unspecified offerings, came to over $594,000. This figure translates into an average of $1,828 for each of the church's 325 households, elevating Desert Cross far above the national average for congregations of the Evangelical Lutheran Church in America.

Yet Steve Holm is far from complacent about his parish. His message in the September 1996 issue of the church newsletter voiced what many members were probably thinking:

> Sometimes on Sunday mornings it feels like I know only about half the people at the service. Many times faces will be familiar but I haven't the slightest notion what names belong to these persons. And if it's that way for me, it's even more so for everyone else! We've lost a lot of that intimacy that was once part of our experience. One long-time member told me last Sunday that as she looked around she scarcely saw anyone that she knew. That's a disquieting feeling when we've thought of church as being family.

Steve Holm saw little chance of recapturing the cozy feelings of earlier times, but he managed to conclude with a hopeful note:

I believe that it's possible for even a large congregation to feel like a family if we can maintain a caring, friendly attitude at worship and continue to expand our small-group ministry. So I pray that we will continue to greet one another with warm smiles and words of welcome.

A visitor immediately senses a dynamism about this church. An illustration is ChristCare Groups, the small-group ministry cited by Holm. By spring 1998, more than 130 adults were involved in 14 groups, with more groups ready to go. Each ChristCare group focuses on the Gospel and Old Testament lessons to be read that Sunday, which determine the subject of the pastor's sermon. All Sunday school groups study the same passages. As Holm puts it, "Everyone in the congregation is working on the same Bible text on a weekly basis." Finance board member Curt Hahn describes his ChristCare experience:

In the group I'm in, we have a time of sharing with one another before the study begins. A lot of what is shared is kind of personal and stays within these walls, so there's a real strong trust there. One of our group members lost his 23-year-old son a short time back and had lost his father six months before. Even though we're not a support group, he says, "'If I didn't have this group here. . . .'"

Dottie Ohe was equally laudatory of her ChristCare group:

For me, I get to see people spiritually, to see where they are through the study we do together. The learning part of all this has been so immense for me I can't even describe it. I feel the growth I've experienced since I've been in my group has been so empowering that it also helps me to feel closer and with more trust towards these other people. And when you add 12 or 14 other people that experience the same thing, that energy is going to expand outward.

The "hunger jar" is an example of that expanding energy. Steve Holm urged Dottie to share its story with me. The jar was placed in the narthex to solicit money for the synod's hunger appeal.

Then at one point, someone just made a snap decision and said, "Why don't we move it up front?" Which only made sense, really. The focus now of offering time is to watch children walk forward and drop their money. You see, everyone is welcome to just go forward and give to the jar–coins, dollar bills, whatever you happen to have. My own kids really look forward to it. And usually, as they go up, people in the pews reach over and whisper, "Here, put this in."

Woody Nieman concurred. "It's a traffic jam! Don't be in their way if you're one of those taking up the offering. You'll get run over!" As a consequence of the resettled jar, Desert Cross became the second-highest church in hunger giving within the ELCA's Grand Canyon Synod. No one foresaw how the custom would catch on. As Dottie remarked,

To me it's so much fun to see these kids who were baptized a few months before. Now they're making their first trek up to the front of the church with money in their hands and dropping it into the jar. At first, they don't know why they're doing it. You'll see a kid come up there with four quarters in his hand. He takes three of them and drops them in there. But he'll look at that last quarter, and sometimes that quarter just goes right back in his pocket! But there's a spirit of life and giving here. That's the point.

A further point is that the hunger jar yielded a total of $8,302 in 1997. These funds went to world hunger, the Oklahoma City Bombing Relief, a local hospital, and to the church's annual Thanksgiving Food Drive. By spring 1998, over $8,000 was collected for Lutheran World Federation's Augusta Victoria Hospital on the Mount of Olives in Jerusalem.

Serendipitous things happen in vital parishes. But they don't happen without a sound organizational base that undergirds stewardship.


## Stewardship and Basic Organization

Steve Holm inherited a parish where key lay leaders "already had pretty full-blown notions of what stewardship was all about." Steve took leadership by introducing an expanded structure of boards and a governing council within the parish.

Perhaps my gift to the congregation, which was kind of ironic because I am not a well-organized person, was to provide a structure that this board or these people could work within to make the congregation aware of needs and responsibilities as well as their opportunities. We pretty well changed the entire structure of the congregation, and now have a stewardship board that focuses on that arena all year long. Six strong people. In fact, we've always had strong people in the area of stewardship.

Besides stewardship, the nine boards that meet regularly include Christian education, congregational life, church property, evangelism, finance, social concerns, worship, and youth. The president of the congregation, working with an executive committee, monitors the work of boards and committees to ensure that their objectives are being met. Overall lay governance lies with the congregational council, made up of all board chairs and the executive committee. Former congregation president Woody Nieman reflected on the effect of this structure:

And the pastor . . . well, Steve doesn't feel like he's the CEO of a corporation where he has to make a bunch of decisions. The structure works. The council is a working unit, and below are the boards, and things are happening. Often the council doesn't even make decisions—it's just information flowing up. The decision-making largely takes place at lower levels. That's why it feels like you're in a smaller church.

The feeling of belonging to a smaller church begins, it seems, the last night of new-member orientation. The nine board chairs present make presentations and often recruit directly. As Nieman said, "Many times they have already wrapped up some of these new members before they have to make a decision because they already know what their interests and talents are." Former stewardship chair Mike Friend, now chair of long-range planning, echoes the idea of small church.

This church has always been small to me, even though we have 800 members. It kind of surprised us here a year ago in some long-range planning sessions. We were told, well, you realize you guys are a large church. We are? We thought we were a small church. That means we've been pretty effective at keeping a small-church environment while we grow. A lot of that is due to the small-group ministry that allows people to feel like they can have an impact. If you go to Grace Community Church here in town, there might be 1,000 in the sanctuary on Sunday. You could see the pastor Monday morning at the supermarket, and he wouldn't know you from Adam. That's why I say to people here, if you really want to feel part of this church, get involved in something, because you're not going to meet a new friend just by sitting next to someone in the pew on Sunday morning. Doesn't happen that way.

The empowerment resulting from this overall structure means that church members feel free to innovate and expand and seek new avenues of ministry through the boards. Examples abound. Since approximately one-third of church members are under 20 years old, youth ministry flourishes. There are events for junior and senior high school students on Sunday, Wednesday, and Friday evenings. Similar planned events now reach youngsters from kindergarten through sixth grade. The youth board helped charter Troop 379 of the Boy Scouts, complete with field trips, camporees, and hikes. ChristCare groups for teenagers allow adults and kids to interact on such topics as peer pressure, moral choices, suicide, and accepting our families. A yearly calendar goes out so that youth and parents can plan their schedules around this array of activities.

Besides sponsoring the ChristCare groups, the evangelism board sees to it that first-time visitors to Desert Cross receive a home visit by an outreach team with packets of information about the church; a welcome table is provided at Sunday worship to dispense information and answer questions. A six-week "Inquirer's Class" is offered three times a year, taught by one of the pastors. Sponsors are assigned to new members to help them assimilate into the Desert Cross community. In fact, the church recently called a part-time ministry coordinator to help with this process of assimilation. Finally, members who have not been present at worship services for a month are phoned and mailed a postcard encouraging their return to worship. At the end of each year, letters are sent to long-term inactive members asking if they wish to remain on the membership roster (their names are removed if there is no response).

## Finding Time

Woody Nieman thinks the congregation "does a superior job of involving people." As throughout the country, families struggle to set priorities for time and activities. Dottie Ohe:

> Where do we find the time? In our family, we have church activities that are mandatory over and above soccer or whatever. We first fit those in, and after that, we fit in other things. Time is limited, and we try to maintain our family time, our worship time. In terms of extracurricular activities that our kids get involved in, well, we try to steer them to church activities. Activities outside of church? We're there right with them. We try to let the kids establish their own priorities, but hopefully we're guiding them toward the priorities we think are important, without dictating to them what they'll be involved in.

Dottie belongs to a "moms' group" made up mostly of professional women who have quit their jobs to stay home with their children. The group support is invaluable:

> It was hard for me to quit my job. But at the same time, knowing that I had that kind of support from the group, it was very helpful. And there are other people cutting back on the frills, I guess, in order to do what we all did. It helps a lot. When we were making that decision at home, I just remember our life was crazy. When we were first married, we were both very active. And that suddenly stopped when we had children. The spiritual part was harder to maintain. We realized at some point that part of it was gone, and without it, the rest was going to fall apart. So I definitely think our decision was based more on family-value issues than on money issues; that's for sure.

Members talked about the volunteering aspect of stewardship coming into play during the spring focus on time and talent–and not just with adults. Kids in confirmation classes are taught about the importance of volunteering: In summer 1998 a group of young people traveled to Mexico and to Lithuania to engage in service projects. Money management also receives attention. The church sponsored a financial seminar, which included suggestions for involving one's children in the financial aspects of stewardship. A book, *Managing Your Money*, was the basis of discussion. Out of the seminar came the notion of talking to children about saving part of their allowance for the church in envelopes set aside for the purpose. Woody Nieman again:

> I'm just amazed at the number of parents in our congregation who talk about giving and stewardship. Take the hunger offering we talked about. Some of that money the kids bring up isn't what they've "robbed" from their parents! It's their own money. They're tithing, in a way. And that's neat to see.

## Stewardship Ideals

Steve Holm sees stewardship as going beyond "the basics" of time, talent, and money.

> There's more to it. It's not necessarily even what is given, but it's rather how you use all of the things that you have. I mentioned to you that I played golf this morning as part of my stewardship of time. And I take that very seriously. Stewardship involves all that is available to me and my use of it in certain specific ways, within the congregation, it involves how we use all those kinds of things within the context of the church. One of the things we try to do here is encourage people, to let them know that everything they do is their stewardship, not just what they give to the congregation. Their work is their ministry, too. The workplace is where they share their gifts with others.

Woody Nieman elaborated:

> In some Lutheran parishes, stewardship always takes a bad rap. It's the committee nobody wants to be on, since you are the ones charged with beating the bushes and shaking people. "They're here for my money again." In a small Lutheran parish I was in back east, the every-member visitation was something to be

dreaded like the plague. Here, it's funny. It's a kind of lack of emphasis, yet a lot of emphasis at the same time. It's a part of everything we do. It's a continual knowledge, an awareness without any pressure that seems to be associated with stewardship. We don't have to go shake out anything from people. Every time we make a need known it's met. And [there's] nothing high-profile about it. It's publicized in the bulletin on Sunday, in the monthly newsletter, and we get responses.

*Do you speak directly on money, Steve?*

Very seldom directly. At the max, maybe once a year. I was told by a parishioner in the very first parish I served in 26 years ago, "Make sure you don't get the dollar sign in place of the cross." I've always kind of remembered that, that people are very sensitive about hearing sermons on money, in feeling like there's some kind of coercion taking place. So we don't do any kind of appeals for money on Sundays in the course of the service. In the biblical texts we use on Sunday, there are plenty of references about our attitude toward material things, our attitude toward our property and other things. So it's very natural just to preach the Scriptures and let them speak; not try to see it as a fund-raiser, though we've done specific fund appeals here. In fact, we're coming up on one.

Woody Nieman:

Yes, but even the fund appeals are tied into a weeklong activity that's very Gospel-centered and very parish-centered.

By 1993, it was clear that the church needed some new buildings and that church debt had to be reduced to accomplish this goal. Desert Cross called on the ELCA's Resident Stewardship Service. Money raised in the campaign was originally earmarked for debt reduction, but in effect it paid for two new buildings. The debt remained, but a new physical plant emerged from the almost $600,000 raised. Nieman reflected on the process:

I think there was a kind of synergy that occurred in the whole thing. We talked at council recently about how we really don't dwell upon the price of something. We don't fritter away money. We're now looking at programs and benefits as we go further down the line. That was not always true. It's a change over the last three years. It's like once you see that you *can* do something, there's a relief to it. I think we've experienced a fundamental change in the congregation's financial structure. It changed with that RSS program three years ago.

Pledging has become an expected feature in the parish. On a regular basis, the pastor estimated, between 150 and 200 household units out of the parish total of 300 turn in commitment cards. The result is continued debt reduction, new buildings, and an increase in paid staff, which, in turn, supports expanded ministries. As Nieman put it, the level of support "seemed to pick up like a turbocharger. Something kicked in and reinforced itself. We always used to run just a little bit under what we were supposed to have."

*Are members asked to pledge proportionately?*

Steve Holm:

> Thirty-five is the average age of the adults here, and then there's their kids. The adults don't know any better. They're far from their parents, not in the Midwest any more, but in a new place. And so they're just learning how to give in this congregation, without any preconceived notions of giving or tithing. And yes, we do talk about tithing as a response to God's blessings. The year before we began the building drive, we challenged folks to increase their giving by one percent. Overall, though, about 25 percent of our families give proportionately.

As is the case in other churches, getting more members involved helps them see the financial needs of the church. Curt Hahn is a charter member of Desert Cross. As chair of its first stewardship committee, he recalls a church member turning down the invitation to pledge two years in a row.

> Then he got on the worship committee. All of a sudden, he was in a position where funds were needed to do some things. He came

to me because I was on council. "Where do we get funds for this?" I said, "Remember when I had to ask about the pledge card? Well, this is the way we plan. Without it we don't know what to fund." That did it. He said, "I'll be pledging this year."

Hahn had served on the synod financial commission as well.

I kept hearing from within the commission how we had to justify where the money coming in was going, show people how their hard-earned dollars are working. We had to let them know what the mission of the church is so they can plug into it. For me, though, I say, my gift is my gift and how it's spent and used–well, if they decide to burn it, that's OK! Now, why is my switch on like that? I don't fully understand it. I can just freely let go and I don't have to see. And by the way, people in this congregation learn as much stewardship from each other as they do from preaching. They see examples of each other as role models since, as in other churches, we do have lay members give talks at worship services in which they outline their experiences with tithing.

## Golfing and Stewardship

Steve Holm is not some casual golfer who escapes to the links when he can. Other pastors, he says, are amazed that he's able to play a couple of times a week and yet have a congregation that is strongly active.

And they wonder how I do that. They say, you must be a really good delegator. To me it just all make sense. Why should I try to do something that's not in my skill area or one of my gifts, when there are all kinds of talented people around who can do it better? Plus I am not a perfectionist. I don't have to see that things are done perfectly. And people in the congregation know that. They have a sense of freedom to try things and do things.

Is golf somehow connected with stewardship? Steve Holm has no doubts:

I think the time I take is good stewardship. One of my jobs as pastor is to provide a model of healthy living for members of my congregation. Healthy living involves a certain economy that includes taking care of self. I make sure I establish boundaries for my time within the congregation that allows me to do things for myself. And what I do is golf because it's totally absorbing for me, thinking about the shots I made previously and am making now. And every Friday, I play with other pastors. At times the bishop joins us. It's time when we can be together and enjoy the fellowship. So for me it's an essential part of my ministry. Oh yes, some of my parishioners are jealous and wish they could be pastors, too, so they could golf! The way my schedule is set up, I do have free time during the day. None of my parishioners would like to have my evening schedules, but they all covet my daily schedules!

Holm's reading and reflecting has taken him far beyond golf as just an absorbing and refreshing game:

The books I've read, like *Golf and the Kingdom*,[1] talk about the mystical elements of golf because once you've attained a reasonable skill in the mechanics of golf, which is not that difficult to do, you discover that playing the game totally involves the mind. Professional golfers will say it's 10 percent mechanics and 90 percent mind. I just enjoy that kind of challenge. Some even say there's within each of us something called an authentic golf swing that seeks incarnation. They say the swing is preexistent and maybe even a merger with the presence of God! Occasionally you get in touch with that, a kind of feeling of ecstasy. To stand on a tee and look at a ball that you have struck with an authentic swing is just an awesome experience. And you remember it. To me it's like standing in front of the burning bush!

The difficulty with golf is that there is so much that interferes with the authentic swing, so much of the world that creeps into our thoughts and minds. In Christianity we teach that surrender is such an important part of a person's life—that's how we completely follow Jesus. You surrender yourself, and in losing your life you find your life. The same thing is true in search of the authentic swing: it's as we lose ourselves that we can connect. Golf is just filled with analogies to the Christian life and to daily living. It's absolutely incredible if you start to think about it.

That's why just about all professional athletes, for relaxation and to expand themselves, will play golf rather than their own sport.

*So how to handle your frustrations is a big part of life?*

Yes. Frustrations, emotions, self-control. The Greeks felt that self-control was the most important of the personal virtues. Nothing tests it more than golf! You learn to live in the moment, to experience the good and the bad and to move on to what's next without remembering what has gone before. This is a process-oriented exercise rather than a results-oriented one. People laugh at me when I talk like this because in American society it's results that count. "What was your score?" they want to know, not whether you had an authentic swing.

# Reflection: Small-Church Spirit, Big-Church Expansion

Desert Cross succeeds in retaining a small-church atmosphere. Its ChristCare groups help to develop a close fellowship among members that generates volunteers and new ideas. The president of the congregation spoke of a synergy expressed on a small scale in the hunger jar and more broadly in congregational support for the building drive and in fresh directions for youth ministry. Mothers deciding to stay at home to raise their children find one another and value the group sharing and support. Welcome teams make a first visit to Desert Cross memorable. These features combine to make Desert Cross a friendly and welcoming church that radiates a firm identity and indeed suggests that lives are being changed here.

Money is seldom mentioned from the pulpit, but financial-management seminars, pledge drives resulting in over half of households pledging, every-home visitations (but not yearly), and rotating membership on committees result in involvements that make the financial needs of the parish evident to participants—a kind of stewardship consciousness-raising that gradually spreads throughout the church's active members. That many adult members are recent migrants to Arizona without historical memories of resistance to pledging is of no small importance.

My first thought on speaking with Pastor Steve Holm was that perhaps he was too "laid back" to be a central figure in this church's dynamism and enthusiastic spirit. I could not have been more wrong. His "golf mysticism" is perhaps the key to his leadership style. Losing himself as he "connects," with that image's biblical echoes of surrendering one's ego supports, worries, pet notions, and projects to follow Christ, Pastor Steve Holm achieves a relaxed stance that effectively gives permission to church members to innovate, deepen community, and take charge.

His leadership is by no means passive, of course. His structural reorganization of the parish boards and committees and the new role of the parish council are enabling changes that help ideas and initiatives emerge and develop from the bottom up. Since I first visited the parish in fall 1996, expansion has continued: the church purchased three adjacent acres for a family-life center to be constructed out of funds raised in a projected 1999 capital and debt-reduction campaign. Besides the part-time coordinator mentioned previously, the music director's post is now full-time. An associate pastor was added to work with youth, aided by a half-time youth coordinator.

The overall result is a truly dynamic congregation that indeed "feels like a small church." I found myself enjoying conversations with the parish lay leaders, whose sense of how far the church had come and of the new directions and goals under consideration generated palpable enthusiasm. They exuded a kind of continual awareness that being a steward percolates into all aspects of life, including one's workplace and the larger Tempe/Phoenix community. This spirit works directly against the individualism and "I'll just take care of my own garden" mentality often associated with suburban American life in the nineties. Desert Cross, I thought, stands as an inspiring "light on the mesas" in the fast-expanding American Southwest.

## CHAPTER 12

# STEWARDSHIP: MEETING THE LONG-TERM CHALLENGE

In the epilogue to *Grant Us Courage*, Randall Balmer, professor of religion at Barnard College, brings a touch of sadness to his musings on mainline Protestantism. After visiting 40 years later a dozen churches designated by *The Christian Century* in 1950 as "great churches," he was not hopeful, nor could he resist comparing them with evangelical churches he had written about in 1989.[1] They, more than mainline churches, "have been better able to resist the ravages of routinization"; the "relentless populism" of their leaders ensures that they "are more attuned to the sentiments of their congregants."[2]

> In the eyes of many Americans mainline Protestants have been so intent on blurring theological and denominational distinctives that they stand for nothing at all, aside from some vague (albeit noble) pieties like peace, justice, and inclusiveness.[3]

Donald Miller, professor of religion at the University of Southern California, is even more critical of mainline congregations in his study of Calvary Chapel, Vineyard Christian Fellowship, and Hope Chapel. As "new paradigm" evangelical churches, they respond better than their mainline counterparts to the needs of "their clientele." More significantly, he believes,

> they are successfully mediating the sacred, bringing God to people and conveying the self-transcending and life-changing core of all true religion. They offer worship in a musical idiom that connects with the experiences of broad sectors of the middle class; they have jettisoned aspects of organized religion that alienate

many teenagers and young adults, and they provide programming that emphasizes well-defined moral values and is not otherwise available in the culture. In short, they offer people hope and meaning that is grounded in a transcendent experience of the sacred.[4]

The 11 churches in this book, I maintain, largely escape these critiques. Rendered vital through their stewardship theologies, programs, and ministries, they appear anything but "routinized" as they find new avenues of outreach. Young families join, and pastors successfully challenge their congregations to give of their resources of time, talent, and money. Worship services are alive; music has often been changed to appeal precisely to the strata claimed by evangelical churches. Pastors are no less attuned to the needs of their congregants for meaning, for healing, and for a sense of the sacred as the growth of adult spirituality, Bible study, and prayer groups amply attests. No member of Acton Congregational Church, First Institutional Baptist, or Northkirk Presbyterian would entertain any doubts as to what his or her church stands for, what its mission is, or whether it is worth generous support.

Irrelevant or moribund? Quite the contrary: The very vitality of these "stewardship churches," I believe, sheds light upon two basic questions: (1) Are critics correct in calling into question the continued usefulness of a stewardship approach today and into the future? (2) Is this approach relevant to renewal and revitalization of mainline churches? Let us consider each of these questions.

1. *"Everybody knows it's about money."* Let us return for a moment to the critics alleging that stewardship has devolved into a pseudo-spiritual synonym for annual fund-raising. Even stewardship advocates incline towards skepticism. Acknowledging the influence of Robert Wood Lynn, consultant Ronald Vallet, former editor of the *Journal of Stewardship*, remarks that the church has been through three stages in the vocabulary of giving: "charity, benevolence, and stewardship. All three of these stages provided ways of talking about faith and money."[5] While supporting the *theology* of stewardship and writing eloquently of its value, Vallet believes that the *vocabulary* of stewardship may be outmoded. "It is clear that a new stage of language to describe giving will emerge in the coming years. It is not yet clear what the changes will be."[6] Both Vallet and Loren Mead agree that the value of the coin has diminished. In fact, Mead, as I pointed out in the introduction, goes much further in his criticism: Stewardship, in becoming "a euphemism for fund-raising," has lapsed into "a

doubletalk . . . genuinely confusing to many laypeople."[7] Moreover, stewardship carries with it a "payback theology," since it suggests we are to repay God "for the good things God has given us."[8] Mead calls for a theology of money and giving that carries more substance.

While I have no intention of wading into a theological debate, I think it clear that pastors, committee chairs, and members of these 11 churches do not find stewardship "confusing," nor do they allow a theology of "payback" to contaminate the notion of making a response to God's goodness. The basic components of stewardship–giving of one's time, talent, and money–are inseparably intertwined in the way stewardship is preached and programmatically expressed. No church member, I think it is safe to say, would hear, perceive, or infer stewardship in any of the 11 churches to be "mainly fund-raising." In fact, pastors and stewardship committee members bend over backward to avoid this restrictive association by setting forth gifts of time and talent as equally important–i.e., discipleship entails the reprioritizing of one's money and time and abilities so as to lay them at the service of the community, its mission and ministries; some also emphasize our stewardship of all creation, of *all* of God's gifts. When they are separated in time–e.g., stewardship of money being emphasized in the fall, time and talent in the spring–this linkage is made explicit: both are set forth as challenges to responsible stewardship. Even the churches that called on their respective denomination's stewardship services or consultants initially for fiscal reasons–All Saints (Wolfeboro), Faith Lutheran, Desert Cross, Arlington Heights–were left in no doubt about the coequal importance of time, talent, and money. Not a single pastor in any of these 11 churches displayed the flag of stewardship as a cloak for "simple fund-raising," not least because each had thought through and preached a theology of stewardship that precluded any such identification.

For me, however, the most central point is that pastors, staffs, and congregations have found stewardship, as they have come to pray about it, talk about it, understand it, and give it time to work, to be a fundamental galvanizing force that works to enhance *and sustain* giving and volunteer energies within the congregation. Stewardship furnishes a theology and a vocabulary enabling pastors and congregational leaders to talk openly to church members about the classically painful topics of money, and in our day of busy two-wage-earner families, giving of time and talents. By no means is this a smooth and easy path. Not every parishioner "buys into the program." We have seen each church struggle in its own way to achieve what it has. "Payback theology"? Virtually absent from their stories is any notion of responding to God as though one were making monthly payments on a loan. In fact, as pastors and stewardship committees responded to my question about the countercultural character of stewardship, clearly evident was the conviction that one major challenge of stewardship lay not so much in awakening a proper sense of thankfulness, as in sensitizing people to the dominance of the consumer society and its handmaiden, the advertising industry. In doing so, they felt, stewardship theology carried the potential of bestowing a freedom from the lure of material wealth that opens the door to true Christian discipleship. This expansive understanding is a far cry from stewardship as fundraising.

2. *Renewal and revitalization.* Stewardship by itself offers no panacea for moribund churches, nor has it assumed the contours of a saving social movement sweeping across mainline Protestantism. Its renewing potential is best assessed, it seems to me, by turning once more to the work of Kirk Hadaway and David Roozen. They believe mainline churches are faced with three choices:

> (1) concede the world to the secular; (2) bring the secular into the church; or (3) claim the secular as a God-given arena for living out one's faith. The first two approaches have led to many of the mainstream's current troubles.[9]

The authors lay their hopes in the third choice, which involves "a return to a highly developed sense of lay vocation" that will lead church members infused with "the vitalizing experience of God in worship" to "affirm the 'sacred' value of faithfully performing 'secular' tasks." But this is precisely what we see in each of these churches, albeit in different degrees. Members do carry an evangelizing spirit into new outreach ministries in their communities, whether it be a night shelter, a delegation meeting with the city council to support a ban on handguns, keeping the local food bank supplied, or building homes for flood victims. Such are the fruits of stewardship commitment. No "retreat from the world" is anywhere to be seen. Furthermore, Hadaway and Roozen envision a reformation in which mainline church leadership—emerging most likely from the ranks of pastors, local church leaders, and seminarians—initiates a quasi-social movement. In coming together, they hope, this new cadre of leaders will share an awareness that we already have the solution among us. It is visible in the way spiritually oriented churches are currently doing worship and ministry. . . . The movement would thus begin as a network of committed reformers [who] will then expand the network, sharing the vision, spreading the theological understanding, and telling the story of churches that embody the essence of the cause.[10]

I respectfully suggest that pastors and churches like the 11 presented in this book come awfully close to what Hadaway and Roozen envision. Dissatisfied with business as usual, they have found their distinctive paths to renewal under the banner of stewardship with a strong sense of vocation to mobilize gifts of time, talent, and money in the myriad ways incarnate in their stories. What I am suggesting is the possibility that "the solution among us" lies in a slightly different social location than that envisioned by Hadaway and Roozen: in local churches like these 11 and their many, many counterparts as yet unsung and unwritten about. Where stewardship takes hold, as it has in these churches, it seems to me that a force for renewal stands ready for mobilization. While further speculation is probably premature, we can summarize what has given these 11 churches their distinctive stamp and lends them the renewal potential I suggest.

## Ingredients of Successful Stewardship

1. *Convinced pastoral leadership.* Stewardship authors are fond of underlining the indispensable role of the pastor. They are absolutely correct. All 11 pastors shared a vision of what stewardship could do and where it could lead the church; that it was eminently worth sticking with, in season and out of season. Here was no magic talisman that could be trotted out for each fall's pledging or budget-raising campaign. As active, smart, and creative as a lay stewardship committee might be, I found each member praising just this vision and involved leadership by the pastor. By no means, they implied, was the pastor simply "handing this all over to us–good luck, everybody. I know you can do it." Each pastor made sure stewardship was a year-round theme nurtured by his persistent encouragement and, often, outright enthusiasm. I think of All Saints (Episcopal) in Pasadena, First Institutional Baptist in Phoenix, Northkirk Presbyterian in Alta Loma, or Christian Church of Arlington Heights, Illinois. Holding the vision up before the congregation is an apt description of the pastor's role.

Each saw stewardship as a defining dynamic of his church and conveyed that to one and all.

The phrase "comfortably delegating" not only fits each pastor, but also struck me as the most salient of the qualities I came to admire. Underlying a willingness to delegate was the conviction that stewardship would work only if it were a collective enterprise, an ongoing process that involved those already on board and kept adding more. Being open to members' suggestions, encouraging and respecting their initiatives while holding individuals and committees and commissions accountable in a supportive fashion was the "CEO style" the pastor adopted. The result of this style of leadership, as Peter Brock and practically every corporation consultant asserts, is to give everyone permission to bring his or her gifts and talents and ideas to the table. These pastors knew, or intuited, that this leadership mode was exactly what taking stewardship seriously meant. It meant the full calling forth of the community's gifts, the personal endowments of each and every member, in a climate of respect animated by a theological vision of who we are and what God calls us to—and that we all thrive when this is happening. We have to keep this dynamism going and surely can't stop now! Perseverance in stewardship was a "must" for each.

When we turn to the stewardship of money, almost every pastor led the way in giving, whether by tithing or a close approximation. I found that congregation members knew this to be true, whether or not the pastor was explicit about it. They said it affected their own giving.

Another phrase this leadership style evoked—one that has virtually achieved cliché status today—was a sense of ownership. Church members praised pastors for precisely this quality of letting go and empowering in Desert Cross, Woodmont, and in both Episcopal churches, but it was present to a notable degree in all 11. I think it accounts in large part for the sense of enthusiasm I encountered in every congregation. "He lets us know this is our church." Exactly.

Finally, all 11 pastors shared a willingness, approaching in some a strong sense of obligation, to talk directly to their congregations about money. A few, like Pastor Rob Page or Father Ed Bacon or Bacon's predecessor, Father George Regas, could be quite confrontive on the subject. Money is an indicator of spiritual health: This seemed to be a conviction shared by several pastors. But in every case, money was brought up fearlessly because of the reigning conviction shared by all pastors that it is a spiritual necessity for each of us to evaluate our attachment to money and wealth. Given the frequently noted reluctance of most pastors to bring up the subject, as we noted in *Money Matters*,[11] this out-front approach is quite remarkable. This is not to say that all church members appreciated having it called to their attention. However, in a local-church context of vital worship and music, expanding ministries, and provision of spiritual-growth opportunities that stewardship helps bring about, members will respond, as we have seen—particularly when it is evident that the pastor's own giving is consistent with his preaching. As a parting note, I cannot help thinking of the spiritual lives of many of the pastors that percolated through the interviews and impressed me deeply. As one church member remarked about her pastor, "He's the real thing."

2. *Ministries and Programs.* All churches have these, but adopting a stewardship approach creates a climate or, as the president of Desert Cross Church put it, a "synergy" in which ideas for outreach and for programs benefiting church members and their families are constantly generated. Sometimes it is the pastor who does the asking, as when Dan Webster of Christian Church of Arlington Heights inquired of young adults at a Sunday service what they thought would attract their peers. A congregation may turn to someone with special talents: I think of Northkirk, with a member trained in discernment of spiritual gifts that helped place people in ministries reflecting their talents. I warmly recall the vibrant spiritual life of First Institutional Baptist and the class in prayer I attended between Sunday services, one of many being held throughout the building at that hour. I closed the story of Woodmont Christian Church by relating the informal service for young families and their children that the new pastor had initiated. "Creative energy" comes to mind. Stewardship brings forth in its emphasis upon time and talent a thrust toward seeking new ways of serving those not yet included. The "institutional stewardship" of First Presbyterian, Fort Worth, yields one example among many related in this book.

3. *Welcoming Ministry and New Member Expectations.* Welcoming as a ministry takes on dynamic forms in several churches—Acton Congregational, Northkirk, St. Paul, and Faith Lutheran, among others. Linked with welcoming, in several cases, is information about what membership in this church means. Here the notion of "strictness" made its appearance. I refer to the policies of some churches to let newcomers know, "Unless you are ready to . . . this may not be the church for you"–e.g., Northkirk. Welcoming, of course, primarily entails a warm reception for inquirers

that makes them feel at home (Desert Cross provides a fine example). In virtually all cases, however, stewardship, since it emphasizes responsibility for what one has been given and for how one responds, leans toward a strict view of the meaning of membership, even in churches representing more liberal denominations like the United Church of Christ and the Episcopal Church.

4. *Enhanced Financial Support.* Stewardship of money is, obviously, the stickiest of issues to preach about. Exhorting the congregation to dig deeper is not fun for any pastor, and all of them echo this sentiment. But a stewardship approach does succeed, the most convincing examples being churches that recently "got on board": All Saints (Wolfeboro) and Faith Lutheran (All Saints' 26 percent increase in three years is indeed impressive!). Growth in regular giving is slow, but it does occur, not least because pastors are no longer reluctant to deal with the issue. Several pastors, including those of both Disciples congregations, Northkirk, Acton, St. Paul, First Institutional Baptist, All Saints (Pasadena), and First Presbyterian, were pleased to let me know that their church was a leading contributor in some respect within the United States or their region, synod, or presbytery. All the churches were strong mission contributors, some outstandingly so.

5. *Stewardship Committee.* This study underlines what most stewardship consultants will advise: The stewardship committee should be just that. It is *not* a finance committee and should not be saddled with this responsibility. Stewardship committees are responsible for growth of stewardship consciousness within the congregation, for helping the pastor plan campaigns for both the fall budget and for increased volunteer support for ministries. They are charged with keeping alive the vision that animated the adoption of stewardship in the first place. They may at times find themselves in tension (preferably a healthy tension!) with the finance committee, most often over fund-raising events which, if frequent, seem to run contrary to the stewardship ideal of all funds coming through regular offerings and pledges (and may well depress the latter). There is no simple formula for working through these tensions, though strong and sensitive pastoral leadership is a key element. Faith Lutheran provides an excellent example of fruitful interaction between the stewardship committee and other committees.

# A Researcher's Reflection

In *Money Matters*, and in *Plain Talk About Churches and Money*,[12] my colleagues and I discussed stewardship because so many pastors talked to us about it. We noted which of our major survey findings seemed correlated with features of a stewardship approach: high levels of parishioner involvement in the church, an evangelical (strict) theology, and giving planned by year, of which pledging is an example. All 11 churches in the present study lean strongly in these directions, of course.

From our interviews with pastors in *Money Matters* came several observations borne out in this research. First, stewardship indeed involves long-term educational challenges, an effort to change deep-rooted values and perceptions about money and church. The sense of struggle coming through in these 11 churches certainly validates this observation. A church like All Saints in Wolfeboro, New Hampshire, having begun stewardship quite recently, provides an example of long-term struggle, as does St. Paul in Columbia, Illinois, in which a newly arrived veteran stewardship pastor knows he has his work cut out for him. Second, with its reiterated biblical base, stewardship truly differs in both purpose and tone from fund-raising, a theme repeated throughout this book. Third, stewardship's focus is on the individual's need to give, not on the church's need to receive. Of course, the two can be integrated, as we have seen, but any predominant stressing of a church's needs at the expense of the stewardship theology of giving will simply kill genuine stewardship. It is precisely this abuse that gave rise to the critiques of stewardship by Mead, Lynn, and Mulder cited in the introduction. All the pastors would agree on this. Finally, the motivation inherent in the stewardship ideal depends on strong faith. Not all church members will rise to these levels of understanding, acceptance, and commitment. Repeatedly in the accounts above, we have seen each church's struggle (particularly those recently adopting stewardship) to break down "the 80-20 principle" by which a relatively small minority shoulders the burdens of both financial support and engagement in ministries and programs. It is little wonder that such respected church consultants as Kennon Callahan advise four years as the minimum time for a stewardship program to begin to take root in a congregation.

Over the course of this research and writing I have come to see stewardship as holistic. In these churches, pastors and stewardship committees, through reiterated association and integration of money with time and talent in a spiritual context, keep stewardship from degenerating into "mere fund-raising." The resulting synergy is what visitors notice, a kind of "crack-ling" that seems to pervade the church office, committee meetings, wor-ship services and music, even the coffee-and-doughnuts hour following a Sunday service where, as I mentioned in the introduction, I was often struck by the enthusiastic comments of congregation members. These were un-mistakable signs, I thought, that these mainline churches simply did not fit the images of churches in trouble, even dying. On the contrary, they were indeed vital, conveying a sense of purpose and a quiet confidence about the future. Here I think of Loren Mead's conclusion to *Financial Melt-down in the Mainline?* He reflects that the financial problem of mainline churches

> is probably caused by our lack of nerve, our fearing to face the
> spiritual dimension of our lives and of our society. The crisis of
> the churches is a call to us to become a community that celebrates
> the presence of God in the midst of life and the things of life.[13]

I am convinced that the congregations I have seen have found their nerve and embraced the spiritual dimension of their lives. They have become communities celebrating God's presence in the midst of lives turning to the work of the Kingdom in worship, gift-giving, and ministry.

APPENDIX

**Interview Guide for Initial Conversation with Pastor**

1. What I am handing to you is a page with a definition of stewardship I have drawn up. Does it pretty much describe stewardship as you understand it?

> An invitation to members of a congregation to commit resources of time and talent and money out of thankfulness and a desire to return God's gifts in order to advance his kingdom in their community and beyond. This invitation may take the form of an organized program and may involve further invitations to pledge and/ or to tithe.

2. How and when did your present stewardship effort/program come about? What got it started?

3. How would you describe its main emphases?

4. Does stewardship here reflect an effort at the level of the presbytery (synod, district, etc.), or is it strictly a local program at this church?

5. Many say it takes years to get across to a congregation the elements of stewardship–that it is very slow going. Would you agree?

6. How do you talk about or present stewardship in your preaching? How often do you preach on this subject? What times of the year?

7. Do you deal with all the elements of stewardship–time, talent, money–at the same time (say, in the fall), or do you treat them separately and at different times of the year?

8. Do you emphasize proportionate giving? How? Is tithing recommended? Is pledging a practice here? For how long? What proportion of households (giving units) actually pledge?

9. Stewardship literature often cautions about reciprocity–if I am generous with God, I will get repaid somehow. Is this an issue you feel you have to deal with?

10. Can you tell me about the relationship of stewardship in this church to each of the following:

    A. Ministries

    B. Liturgy

    C. Music

11. Does stewardship, as practiced here, embrace all giving, including capital needs? Are special collections taken for various needs; e.g., for missions, apart from regular giving?

12. Has average regular giving in the congregation increased since stewardship was introduced? If so, by how much?

13. How are members of the stewardship committee nominated/elected/chosen? How long is the normal term on the committee?

14. Do you see stewardship as countercultural? If so, how?

15. Are endowments and planned giving emphasized? If so, are they treated as part of overall stewardship here?

# NOTES

## Introduction

1. Robert Wood Lynn, "Why Give?" in Mark Chaves and Sharon L. Miller, eds., *Financing American Religion* (Walnut Creek, Calif.: Alta Mira Press, 1999), 61.

2. Lynn, "Why Give?," 61.

3. Loren B. Mead, *Financial Meltdown in the Mainline?* (Bethesda, Md.: The Alban Institute, 1998), 88.

4. Mead, *Financial Meltdown*, 88

5. John M. Mulder, "Faith and Money: Theological Reflections on Financing American Religion," in Chaves and Miller, 160.

6. Mulder, "Faith and Money," 160.

7. Dean R. Hoge, Charles Zech, Patrick McNamara, and Michael J. Donahue, *Money Matters: Personal Giving in American Churches* (Louisville: Westminster John Knox Press, 1996).

8. Assemblies of God do not use the term "stewardship," but with their membership norms of tithing and active participation, they resemble mainline Protestant and Catholic churches with strong stewardship programs.

9. Jackson W. Carroll, Carl S. Dudley, and William McKinney, eds., *Handbook for Congregational Studies* (Nashville: Abingdon Press, 1986).

10. Nancy T. Ammerman, Jackson W. Carroll, Carl S. Dudley, and William McKinney, eds., *Studying Congregations: A New Handbook* (Nashville: Abingdon Press, 1998).

11. Peter Block, *Stewardship: Choosing Service Over Self-Interest* (San Francisco: Berrett-Koehler Publishers, 1993), 6.

12. Block, *Stewardship*, 8.

13. Block, *Stewardship*, 22.

14. Block, *Stewardship*, 23.

15. C. Kirk Hadaway and David Roozen, *Rerouting the Protestant Mainstream: Sources of Growth and Opportunities for Change* (Nashville: Abingdon Press, 1995). The points in this section are summarized from chapter three, 55-72.

## Chapter 1

1. The phrase "faith-promise" has its roots in the Abrahamic covenant related in the 15th chapter of the Book of Genesis. Today it is often synonymous with "pledging"; e.g., the pastor of Northkirk Presbyterian Church (chapter 8) refers to the pledge card as the "faith-promise card." Its particular use in Acton Congregational Church is simply an extension of this meaning.

## Chapter 4

1. A social scientist will recognize the phenomenon of group "effervescence" described by one of sociology's founders, Emile Durkheim. Intense group involvement ritually expressed generates feelings of being caught up in the larger social entity (in this case, the church) and gives rise to strong loyalties and creative energies.

## Chapter 5

1. Laurence Iannacone, "Why Strict Churches are Strong," in Thomas E. Dowdy and Patrick McNamara, eds., *Religion North American Style* (New Brunswick: Rutgers University Press, 1997), 63-64.

## Chapter 6

1. "Ebenezer Scrooge Would Feel at Home Here," *Concord Monitor*, December 23, 1995, A-1 and A-6.

## Chapter 8

1. Promise Keepers is an evangelical organization of men whose mission statement is "A Christ-centered ministry dedicated to uniting men through vital relationships to become godly influences in their world."

## Chapter 10

1. The ELCA's office of Resident Stewardship Service, originated by an ELCA predecessor body some 40 years ago, was discontinued March 1, 1999.

## Chapter 11

1. Michael Murphy, *Golf in the Kingdom* (New York: Dell, 1972).

## Chapter 12

1. Randall Balmer, *Mine Eyes Have Seen the Glory: A Journey into the Evangelical Subculture* (New York: Oxford University Press, 1989).

2. Randall Balmer, *Grant Us Courage: Travels Along the Mainline of American Protestantism* (New York: Oxford University Press, 1996), 145.

3. Balmer, *Grant Us Courage*, 148.

4. Donald E. Miller, *Reinventing American Protestantism: Christianity in the New Millennium* (Berkeley: University of California Press, 1997), 3.

5. Ronald E. Vallet, *Stepping Stones of the Steward: A Faith Journey Through Jesus' Parables*, second edition (Grand Rapids: Eerdmans, 1994), 160.

6. Vallet, *Stepping Stones*, 160.

7. Loren B. Mead, *Financial Meltdown in the Mainline?* (Bethesda, Md: The Alban Institute, 1998), 87.

8. Mead, *Financial Meltdown*, 87.

9. C. Kirk Hadaway and David Roozen, *Rerouting the Protestant Mainstream: Sources of Growth and Opportunities for Change* (Nashville: Abingdon Press, 1995), 115.

10. Hadaway and Roozen, *Rerouting the Protestant Mainstream*, 120.

11. Dean R. Hoge, Charles Zech, Patrick McNamara, and Michael J. Donahue, *Money Matters* (Louisville: Westminster John Knox Press, 1996).

12. Dean Hoge, Patrick McNamara, and Charles Zech, *Plain Talk about Churches and Money* (Bethesda, Md.: The Alban Institute, 1997).

13. Mead, *Financial Meltdown*, 126.